PEACH STATE PRECISION

The Sportsman's Guide to Hunting Georgia Whitetail Deer

Nathan Dallas

Contents

Foreword

Success requires a solid plan. An elite deer-hunting strategy demands focused education, dedicated practice, and diehard discipline. If you want to be a better whitetail hunter, you need all three of these elements. This book will prepare you for the high-level performance you desire as a hunter. After reading this guide, you will possess the knowledge you seek. You will know how and when to use the insights to gain a significant advantage. Knowledge, coupled with endurance, will prove to be a winning combination for your hunting career.

This book is a gift. The project was born out of a desire to share. Hunting Georgia deer over the years has granted me many awesome memories, thrilling adventures, and so much peace of mind. It's been good for my character and good for my soul. Whether you are brand new to the sport or a seasoned veteran of the tree stand, I am confident that this guide will make you a better hunter. By avoiding mistakes, and having a method to learn more efficiently, we inevitably get to any goal faster. Every skill we learn in life is a process and a journey. Acquiring those skills certainly take time. However, if you have a mentor, it takes much less effort to cultivate a higher level of success. If you allow me to be that mentor, I believe that your journey will be accelerated and you will arrive at your goal much quicker. Let's do this!

CHAPTER 1
The Georgia Challenge

Whitetail hunting in Georgia is tricky, to say the least. It's vastly different from the often manufactured, highly edited, and tediously re-enacted scenes that you see on TV. Beyond the fact that you can't believe everything you see, most of the top shows are filmed hundreds of miles from the Peach State. These hunts take place in alien worlds that are entirely foreign to what we are accustomed to hunting at home in the warm, southeastern corner of the country. On our home turf, the animal size, the herd numbers, the deer behavior, the terrain, the food sources, the tactics, and the results are all different than what we see on the Saturday morning shows. It's important that we differentiate what seems to work in TV-land, and what realistic Georgia hunting is all about. In our state, bruiser bucks are difficult to find and extremely challenging to kill. If you want to be successful in taking an elusive Georgia giant once, you need to get a little lucky. If you want to bag big bucks every year, you must be smart, calculated, disciplined, precise, and also a little lucky.

There are a few habits that must be avoided, and a few others that must be religiously practiced. This book will clearly lay out those items. I have learned most of these practices the hard way, by making heart-breaking mistakes, failing, and gaining valuable and educational on-the-job experience. I have spent over two decades in the southern woods, and I am writing this for one simple reason: That is, that no one else has written a comprehensive, Georgia-specific guide yet. I sincerely believe that it will benefit hunters to have such a manual. I wish I had a compilation like this 20 years ago.

I'm confident that the information in this book will increase your success rates. You will see more deer and better quality deer by following and honing these principles. Whether you are just wading into this heart-pounding sport, or have trudged 10,000 miles through the woods in your knee-high boots and lucky camo cap, there will be a few things that you can use. This information is about practical, proven methods for whitetail hunting success. There is no reason to fill pages with extra information just to add volume. We will move steadily and swiftly from one topic to the next, highlighting the strategies that work and some that typically don't.

The tips, tricks, and staples I mention for Georgia can be used in any state, and will certainly be helpful in all of them. You will become a better local whitetail hunter and can use the expertise all across the country. Just know that what an outfitter teaches you to kill a monster in Texas, Iowa, or Illinois may not be useful at all on the Georgia red clay. Furthermore, it may be the very thing that ruins your chance on your local lease. Our deer are smarter, more alert, and much more skittish than in other places. For mature bucks, it's exponentially more so. They spook faster and have a much keener memory than deer in other parts of the country. It's hard to kill a Georgia monster. Just know that if you learn how to consistently kill trophy white-tails here, you can kill them anywhere.

Before we launch into this journey, I want to challenge you to do the hardest thing for a hunter to do. That is, to consider that you may be doing some things incorrectly, or at least insufficiently. I know that some of you have been hunting for years. Just entertain the idea that you may pick up some awesome tricks to add to your hunting arsenal. You may also need to consider discontinuing some of your traditional methods as well. Try to set pride aside and just have open ears to listen. I am not trying to boast, gloat, or discipline anyone. I just want to share valuable insights.

Sometimes we keep doing the same things over and over and fail to recognize that they aren't working, or that perhaps there is a better way. I find that many hunters do what other hunters do, or what they hear other hunters talk about doing. This is often true, regardless of the credibility or lack of results from the model. If a sportsman talks loud enough, it seems that many are willing to listen. Stop to think about the people you know that kill big bucks, year after year. These are the folks we should be seeking out. Coincidentally, those deer whisperers are often the ones that speak the least. Bagging one big buck several years ago may be blind luck, but an annual wall-hanger after wall-hanger for a decade straight is not. We need to be good students and need quality mentors in all aspects of life. Hunting is no exception. Talk to the folks who are the most successful. Ask for help. Better still, ask them to come hunt with you so you can learn directly from them. People accuse me all the time of being the "luckiest son of a gun" they know when it comes to hunting. They will point out that they put in more hours in the tree than me, spend more energy, effort, and money, and that I'm the lucky one that always comes out of each season with a trophy. The odd thing is that very few hunters will ask me to teach them what I know. I may be a little lucky, but they still don't consider that I may have been a better student over the years and that I may know some valuable insights and strategies. It's much easier to call someone else lucky than it is to admit that we aren't that good at something.

The truth is that nowadays, I do spend less time, effort, and money than most of the guys hunting around me. I work smarter, not harder. It's also true that I enjoy repeated success in the field, and often, many other hunters around me don't seem to do the same. The irony is that many of my peers have much better property to hunt than I do, more time, and greater resources to dedicate to it. I love hunting, but owning multiple businesses and having five young children at home keeps me pretty busy. It's harder than ever to find time to scout, plant, hang stands, monitor activity, and hunt trophy bucks. It's also hard to get them in range with little people at my side ineffectively trying to be quiet. (We'll get there one day.) To be successful, I must be very efficient, productive, and tactically precise. Make no mistake though; I have put in the time over the years—tons of it. I have messed up a lot of hunts and ruined many prime opportunities. That intense learning continues today. I learned most valuable lessons the hard way, and have made just about every mistake in the book. I am still amazed each year at how much more there is to know about deer behavior and why they do what they do. The key is keen observation and continued adaptation. We must always continue to learn and become better. Become a lifetime student and be deliberate about it.

If you aren't successful in the woods, it may not be a bad lease. It might just be you! It's easy to make excuses and deny the possible reality. It may be the way you smell, the way you move around the property, the way you hang stands or a hundred other variables. If you are in a hunting club with six people and the same woman kills the biggest buck every year, she may be more than lucky. She just might be the best hunter. She likely has the knowledge and skill set that you can use too. It's best to drop the, "that must be nice" attitude and the assumption that you are unlucky. Instead, figure out how to do it right. Then you can reap the rewards and satisfaction that comes from killing big whitetails. I have killed big bucks on over-pressured public land, crowded leases, and even farms that were considered worthless for hunting.

To be a high success-rate hunter, you have to put in a great deal of tree time. We must remain attentive, in the stand and on the trail, for years. Learning deer behavior and body language can only come from experience and hundreds of hours of observation. Predicting the next pattern for a deer herd, or anticipating the next minuscule, critical body turn while a deer is feeding comes with the education gathered from devoted, stealthy observation. With that said, the information in the following chapters will function like jet fuel for your hunting career journey. It will give you more opportunities to watch and study live deer in front of you. We all need experience, but with the right manual, the learning track is faster, more intense, and more valuable. My goal is to provide that for you right here. Making the right moves is one important variable. Avoiding the wrong moves is probably the greater one. Let's dive in.

CHAPTER 2
One Simple Goal

I want to take just a minute to lay out what I think is an important foundational principle. There is a valuable mindset that I think is superior to possess when discussing hunting strategies. It's pretty simple, but I think uncommon to many hunters. Please keep this one goal at the forefront:

Instead of trying to manufacture success, strive to eliminate failure.

In other words, let's focus on preventing mistakes, rather than trying to create genius. Most of the time, if a hunt is busted, it's because of a bad move, not just bad luck. If a big buck is harvested, it's usually because a critical error was avoided, not because you made something magical happen.

Deer do what they do, all year, as long as we don't mess it up. When we aren't bothering them, deer continue their smooth routine in the woods every day.

In contrast, when we are around, they change their behavior. If they change behavior based on us, we have made a mistake. The plan should always be to sneak in, undetected, and allow deer to do what they already want and expect to do. Rarely are you going to convince a mature deer to travel over a ridge, leaving the secure bottom he prefers, to investigate a manufactured event that you want him to see. You've got to get into where he wants to be and do so with undercover, sniper-like precision. If you do this without messing up, you will find him eventually.

No magic product will guarantee success. Remember, the guy on TV and the gal on the packaging in the hunting aisle is paid to promote. If there were a special, gotta-have-it tool that produced amazing results every time, we would all know it and pay any price for it. It doesn't exist. You will see a lot of products in the B-roll footage that is recreated and staged on the hunting shows but won't see too many of these things in the footage when the deer is actually in view. We will cover a few things that help and are certainly advantageous to use, but the only plan that produces consistent results is to learn deer behavior, how to find them, and then how to get to them without messing it up. Avoiding tactical errors is the real key to all of this.

We don't want to invite the deer into our house for dinner and try to convince him that we are a nice people. He's too smart and suspicious for that. We want to sneak into his bedroom, hide in the closet, and then wait for him to coast into his daily routine. It's against a deer's instincts to run out into the middle of a field after hearing a nontypical sequence of deer calls.

Good hunters wear many hats. They learn to think not only like a deer, but like a Cherokee Indian, a natural predator, and a Navy Seal, all at the same time. An American Indian with a longbow wouldn't stalk without thinking where to place his foot on each step when walking down a deer trail in pursuit. Seal Team Six finds their target, studies him and his patterns, monitors the surroundings, but waits until the timing is right before moving in. One wrong move ruins the mission. Once the call is made to move, they do so with razor-sharp accuracy, make no mistakes, and come out successful. This is the way we need to approach big buck hunting in Georgia.

CHAPTER 3
Scent Matters

We have a lot of ground to cover in this book, but I think we should start with the most critical items first. Number one on the list (and will always be) is scent. You've likely already heard that a deer's number one line of defense is his nose. This is absolutely true. Every deer relies on its sense of smell to survive and will trust their nose over everything else. If you mess up the scent equation, the game is over. It's critical. When a big buck smells you, he's gone. This is an absolute in Georgia, and in contrast to some other states' deer, he's not likely coming back anytime soon. He may never come back to that spot again if he is suspicious of your scent.

Not only is your scent the most important topic, but it is also the most complicated. It's not complicated to understand, but it's nearly impossible to execute perfectly. We will explore wind, stand placement, travel, and other topics that will all be heavily influenced by scent. For now, let's focus on one subset at a time. The first category under the scent topic is that of eliminating as much human scent as possible.

MANAGING HUMAN ODOR

Hunters ask the same question all the time. **What kind of cover scent should I use?** If you ask vendors at a hunting expo, you will probably get 50 answers, and I'm sure they will eagerly sell you all of them and swear by their claims. I can simplify the answer for you and emphatically tell you the truth. The best cover scent is none. The goal is not to smell like a fox, a coyote, a doe in heat, or a pine tree.

<u>**RULE #1**</u>: **The goal is to smell like nothing**. The intent is to eliminate human scent, not add more aromas on top of human scent. If you smell like a human that a bobcat urinated on, the buck will not forgive you for trespassing and prance into the food plot, stopping perfectly broadside at 40 yards, giving you a clean kill shot. Furthermore, we don't know that any mammals' urine that has been trapped in a bottle for 243 days still smells correctly. Even if it does, it's not necessarily helping you. Think about it. If you played basketball with nine other men for an hour, sweating, panting, and colliding, but you put on some nice perfume afterward, you just smell like an athlete with complex body odor wearing cologne. It doesn't cover or cancel out the scent already present. It only adds a more complicated, smelly, and confusing olfactory cocktail. If you manage to smell like nothing,

there is no need to try to smell like something else. Luckily for modern hunters, we have weapons for the human scent dilemma.

RULE #2: **Every time you enter the woods, use scent eliminator spray.** This is the rule whether scouting, planting, checking cameras, hunting, or tracking. Hunting is a big business, and fortunately for us, many companies hire really smart chemists and biologists to make these magical field sprays. They work on a cellular level to break down molecules that hold human odor. Trust me. They work and make a huge difference! Do not forfeit using modern technology when it comes to scent eliminating sprays. This one trick alone will dramatically increase your success rates.

If you effectively remove human scent, there is no need to use cover scent. Why smell like a bottled, synthetic, rotten skunk? Just smell like nothing instead. I know what you are thinking, let's eliminate human smells, then add favorable deer smells. The problem is that if you use scent eliminator first, then you spray something else over it, now you have a chemical reaction that is changing the properties of the "good scent" too. What are they really smelling now? Another question we must ask is this: Does a bottled, doe-in-heat scent from last year in Ohio smell like a Georgia doe in heat now? I don't know the answer, and I have never had a buck sit down for an interview to clarify it either. I am convinced that cover scents, as well as buck lures, will hurt you more times than they will help you. For every rare story of the buck coming right down the path where you dragged your scent lure, there are dozens of times where you never saw him because his nose detected something he didn't like.

If you smell like nothing, you can get around more live deer. A real, live, doe in heat under your stand will be the best attractant for your buck. Guaranteed! I will stake my reputation on that. If you insist on using attractants, get some tarsal glands from a recently killed deer from your local deer processor. If you do this, handle the parts carefully. Use rubber gloves and keep them in a sealed bag. Don't contaminate them with human odor by over-handling. If you use this route, a musky rutting buck or a doe in heat will be good choices. These actual, fresh, non-processed scents can be a powerful tool. They can be messy and quite smelly too. I would only use them for a day or two. When not in use, keep them in a sealed bag in a cooler or the fridge. If it's the fridge where you keep food, use an extra bag and warn your spouse or other roommates not to open it.

I'll share an amazing story from a recent kill last season to support my claim of the power of real scent glands. I was hunting a distant farm that has been very well managed for over a decade. It's an awesome place, and there is always a chance to score big. It was peak rut, and the signs were all pointing to a great weekend. Activity was high, and I blocked off three days of work to capitalize on the timing and weather. There was one location, in particular, that was on fire, and the conditions were right to move in for an opportunity. As good fortune may have it, I killed my 141-inch monster buck on the first afternoon hunt.

The wind setup was favorable for me to get on the hot stand and everything was magic. The does showed up and hung around for a while. My bruiser swayed in, directly downwind of the does, and he gave me a few quick seconds to close the deal. That was awesome, but the more impressive scent show happened the next morning. Both of my buck tags were now exhausted. I decided to hunt the next morning to do some recon for my hunting buddies and to hopefully bag a doe. I always take several does off this farm to help with the management plan, and will donate the processed meat to a local soup kitchen if my freezer is full. I watched bucks running does all morning. There was a lot of action, and the deer were very active. If possible, I wanted to wait until I was almost ready to leave to shoot a doe. Finally, about the tenth deer I saw was a mature doe. She stopped at 140 yards and offered a perfect shot. I connected with the 25-06, and she ran 15 yards and fell, still in sight. I waited in the stand for 45 more minutes for my ride to pick me up. During that 45 minutes, a new buck trotted straight to her about every 15 minutes from downwind. Three different bucks picked up the scent, walked right into view, and then walked circles around her a few times and stood over her. The truck finally returned to pick me up, and the third buck scampered off when it arrived. We departed to gather the rest of the hunters and get their reports and returned 30 minutes later to pick up the doe. When we arrived, another buck was standing over her, and yet one more was lingering about 20 yards away. FIVE separate bucks in 90 minutes arrived to check out this doe because of the powerful scent she was emitting. If I had not filled my tag already, I would have used those fresh scent glands for the next two hunts and probably had a serious advantage.

Let's move back to the original proposition. That is, to smell like nothing. **Use scent eliminating spray on everything.** It is very important to cover your boots, top and bottom. It's also important to spray your pants. This is because everywhere you walk can be contaminated by scent. Every tree, briar, bush, or grass patch that you graze against will be affected if you don't plan ahead. Some people walk to the stand, then spray down, only thinking of the time they are in the stand. The travel in and out is equally important. Don't neglect to cover all the bases. Think of it this way for a visual representation: Imagine that I cover you in bright orange, wet paint and then you must walk to your stand. 30 minutes later, I am going to send someone to find you. How much paint did you leave on the grass, bushes, and on the trail? This is an analogy that is good to remember when pondering scent. We must travel carefully and methodically. Don't walk through areas that will leave lots of paint clues. Every time you brush or scrape against anything in the woods, there is a potential to leave some scent (paint) there. A good detective could process all the clues and determine where you are hiding. A big buck can too. His nose will tell him where you were, when you were there, and where you were likely headed. Don't give him any clues.

If you don't spray everything as I recommend, be sure to cover your high, rubber boots. This is a minimum practice every trip into the hunting grounds . . . Every time! This goes for scouting, planting, feeding, and checking cameras too. If your budget allows, spray every article of clothing, including gloves and hats — the boots are just the minimum requirement. Also, tuck your pants into the boots when traveling on foot.

What about soaps, deodorants, and shampoos? In short, I'm a fan. Use any scientifically proven means possible to eliminate human scent. I typically shower with scent eliminator just before leaving to hunt. I use the body soap, shampoo, deodorant, laundry detergent, and the field spray. I think the shampoo is probably the most important of the three because hair holds scent so well. Always wear a hat and a face mask of some sort when in the stand. Your head and hair emit a ton of detectable scent.

What about special clothes? I may catch some scrutiny for this one, but I will tell the truth. **I don't think most "scent eliminating" clothing is worth the money.** They are expensive. They certainly can't hurt anything, so if you have the money, go for it. I support using all effective tools available to us. However, if you do purchase the suit, don't expect it to fix all of your scent problems. You will still need to care for it meticulously. If you don't have a special suit, don't sweat it. I've got you covered.

Here's the scoop. There are many ways that special fabrics can help with scent. Some use charged carbon, some use other minerals, and some use antimicrobial properties that kill or prevent bacteria. Some of these products use carbon-impregnated fabric that is supposed to absorb scent molecules. This may be true in theory, but the function is temporary, and the carbon must be recharged to be able to take up scent on repeated use after you have owned it for a while. The problem here is that your mud-room dryer may not get hot enough to do this effectively. Many people have refuted the legitimacy of hunting claims of carbon clothing. There are plenty of articles that support or deny the effectiveness of these products. There are even some lawsuits about false product claims on some of them. I encourage you to do research and decide for yourself. New technologies are emerging all the time, and the products do get better and more effective. As they advance, they also tend to get more expensive.

Much of the newer technology is focusing on anti-microbial functions instead of scent absorbing carbon. The antibacterial chemicals in these types of clothing are supposed to kill the bacteria on your skin that causes odors. The problem with that is that cigarette smoke, truck exhaust, and the smell of your morning coffee and venison sausage biscuit might not be affected by these. I can tell you from my own experimental research in a college chemistry lab that most anti-bacterial products work poorly unless they are soaking wet in the chemicals for a long while. There are many new fabric innovations out there, but mostly because there is a massive market willing to pay big bucks for it. The new products are not really capable of showing dramatic results just yet. They may partially work, and they may get better in time, but I do not use a so-called scent blocking or scent-eliminating suit myself. What has been proven effective is using scent-eliminating spray to treat your clothing.

I can tell you that regular camo can perform success-fully with proper washes, sprays, and preparation. If you have money to spend, get the suit if you want one. If you are the hunter who has everything else, go for it. As I said, use every tool you can to eliminate scent. Just don't expect a jacket to cover careless mistakes. Even if you have the suit, you still need to follow the other tedious protocols laid out in this book. If you plan to use an antibacterial product, I would recommend buying it in a base layer that makes direct contact with your skin instead of a super expensive outer coat. That way, if it does actually work, it's working at the right level. Remember, you will still need to treat the outer layers too. Whether you wear dollar store camouflage or premium brands, I can give you a winning method to make them all work for you.

How should I care for my hunting clothes? This is a three-step process. 1. Proper washing. 2. Adequate storage 3. Correct Usage. The washing is easy. Put all of your hunting outerwear, and all of your potential base layers, in the washer and use a scent eliminating detergent to clean them. If your normal daily laundry at home is washed using a scented detergent, I would run an empty load with the scent eliminator first to purge the system. After the purge, wash your clothing using the same odor fighting hunting detergent. You cannot be too careful. Dry them without a fabric softener, or use one with the same scent destroying functions. Do not use a regular laundry fabric softener for your hunting clothes. Many people still prefer to dry their hunting gear outside in the sun the old-fashioned way, and I'm sure that's fine too. Once your hunting wear is clean and dry, you should spray your hands and your current shirt (which they will touch while carrying) with the normal scent-eliminating field spray and immediately transfer them to your hunting clothing "safe bag" or box. Do not lay them on the rug or the sofa in the living room to fold. If you are a neat freak and need to fold them, do it outside. Every second you are in the house your clothing is soaking up airborne molecules that are foreign to the deer woods. As far as the "safe bag" to store your gear, you have a few options. If you use a regular garbage bag, be sure that it is unscented. If you use a canvas duffel bag, spray the interior and exterior before putting the clothes in. There are specific bags made by hunting companies that prevent scents from traveling through the fabric. I prefer a standard, snap-top, plastic storage box for my gear. I have several boxes for various conditions and temperatures. Quickly put the clean stuff into the container, and seal it. This box or bag is now a sacred tabernacle that needs to be safeguarded from contamination. Many of the old-timers where I grew up would hang their clothes outside the evening before going hunting so they could "air out." I'm sure this helps some, but if you are protective of your box, you shouldn't need to do this. If you still want to hang the clothes out, be sure to do it far enough away from smoke, people, pets, car exhaust, etc. Be forewarned, putting on the aired-out clothes that are now 25 degrees on the chilly morning of the hunt is no fun. It can also affect your core body temperature and make for an uncomfortable hunt. I keep my treated, sealed box inside the night before so I can stay nice and toasty.

Now that we have a clean, unscented supply of clothes, we are ready to hunt, right? Easy trigger, there are a few things we need to think about before jumping into the coveralls at 5 a.m. Some of you may already think this scent thing is overkill, but you really can't be too careful. This is likely the single biggest determinant of your success or failure in the tree stand. I want you to consider a few more things here. If you put on your meticulously preserved clothes at home and then sit at the local diner to eat, and then ride in the truck for 40 minutes, you are introducing foreign smells into the fabric that you so carefully protected. Your truck seat smells like people . . . Maybe even stinky people. You don't want it touching your pants. You don't want your hat smelling like the breakfast that you just ate either. I have never seen bacon or waffles walking into view on any of my trail cameras. That's not a natural smell that the deer will appreciate. Here is the solution. Don't worry. You don't have to drive naked. Put on the scent-free base layer—or layers if needed—but keep as many things in the safe bag or box as possible. Once you arrive at the spot where you get out of the truck, spray the layer you are wearing and then get fully dressed over it, in the field. Tailgate dressing is the method of choice. Go straight from your safe box to wearing the gear outside. Then you will spray the top layer again too. If you haven't already realized it, I blast through gallons of this stuff each year.

We have effectively covered the topic of clothing preparation, but what about boots? Boots are pretty simple. **High boots made of rubber are what works**

best. Cloth based, agile hiking shoes may be necessary for the hills of Montana, but in Georgia, probably not. I put a lot of miles on my boots and do a lot of on-the-ground, spot-and-stalk style hunting too. I still wear my high, rubber boots because of the distinct advantage they offer for scent control. Try on a few pairs at the store and get some that are comfy and QUIET. Some rubber is squeaky, and some soles are too rigid to walk quietly. Be selective and find the right pair. This is one area of the store where you will probably get what you pay for. Spray your boots down with your field spray just like the rest of your gear. Don't forget to spray the bottom! The surface that contacts the ground, grass, and leaves is the most is critical. Don't hold back when spraying the boots. Get them visibly wet. Tuck your pants legs into them before walking into the timber or beside the food plot. This ensures that the material touching most of the ground cover is rubber. More specifically, rubber that has been de-scented. Double protection is good. If you do not pay attention to this step, you will most definitely leave an unfavorable scent trail everywhere you step. Every blade of grass you touch can leave a clue to your presence. If you leave 1,200 scent clues over 1,200 steps from the truck to the stand, the buck will likely sniff you out and stay far away. You will think the deer weren't moving that day and never know that he actually busted you from the very beginning of the hunt.

These fundamental steps for scent control are critical. These are not negotiable and should become standard daily practice. We will discuss more on scent management, stand placement, and human movement later on in the book.

WIND

Wind can be the most frustrating and challenging factor that affects your hunting. In contrast to other parts of the country, Georgia wind varies from day to day, and sometimes even from hour to hour. It will affect where we sit, how long we sit, and how we get there. It will affect the deer movement patterns and determine your next step on each hunt. Lastly, it can be the knockout blow that ruins your day or even your season. We are still talking about the ever critical scent factor, but now we move from automatic, robotic, repeated, prevention processes for scent elimination to a more strategic and variable game plan. A good hunter is agile and able to adapt to the current situation and avoid potential scent trouble.

We want to be as scent-free as possible, but we will always maintain some level of human smell. We still sweat and most certainly have to breathe. There is no way to be totally free of human scent. We are a scent factory. If a big Georgia buck is downwind from you for any period of time, he will likely smell you. Even if we follow all the steps of prevention, it will still happen if he gets in the right (or wrong) spot. Keeping this in mind, we must use the wind wisely, always respecting the deer's nose and instincts. We don't need to give that bruiser buck, or his lady friends, any reason to be alarmed and behave differently. Remember, we always want them to behave naturally and do what they do, without interruption.

If you don't already have an oversized, printed satellite photo of your hunting tract, get one. Modern technology gives us amazing resources like Google Earth, handheld GPS devices, and phone apps that will give us unbelievably accurate satellite images. Once you have a big copy printed out, laminate it or hang it behind a glass or Plexiglas sheet so that you can use a dry-erase marker to make notes on it. Draw a legend on the map showing true North. Place dots on it to show all of your stand locations and hunting spots. Mark the roads, firebreaks, food plots, and your possible travel routes too. The night before the hunt, and again the morning of, determine the forecasted wind direction. This could be found on the local weather station, on a cell phone app, or by way of the old finger licking trick outside. I like wind-checker powder that comes in a bottle too. Grab some at the hunting store. I keep it in my pocket during every hunt to check for even the slightest changes in wind direction. After establishing the wind forecast, draw a big arrow on the map with a dry-erase marker showing the wind direction for the day. Now we have a visual picture of what is happening outside with the wind. It amazes me that some hunters will pick a stand location a week in advance based on emotion or trail camera pictures, and never consider the wind. It shocks me that some people never stop to check. No wonder they can't see big bucks. When I hear someone say that they are going to a certain stand, days in advance, I know they are a novice.

The first thing to do once the farm and wind direction are in front of you is to eliminate stands that are off limits that day. If the hot food plot, acorn bottom, or the beaten down trail that you want to hunt is downwind from the stand where you want to sit, it's out! No questions asked. If the wind is wrong for a stand, DO NOT GO IN THERE. I don't care if you have 300 pictures of "El Gigante" on the trail camera this week, DO NOT GO IN THERE with the wrong wind. Do you see the text in all caps? I am now yelling at you. This is important. You usually only have one opportunity to kill a Georgia giant. Don't blow it on an emotional whim, a careless impulse, or a poorly thought-out decision with bad wind. Wait until the conditions are favorable to use your lucky spot. This takes patience and discipline. Now that some stands are eliminated, look at the available options left on the map and start considering the best option for the hunt. Pick a stand that will allow deer to move upwind of where you will be sitting. (This is common sense for many of you hunting elites, I know. Stick with me; there will be some good stuff coming for you too.)

Many people will pick the right stand for the actual sit, but neglect to pick the smart route for the trek from truck to stand. What I mean is this, many hunters walk through key areas on the way to the stand, laying down scent that will hurt their chances. They only think of the final destination, which is the stand where they will ultimately sit for two hours. Others still will get it almost right, avoid walking directly through a key area, but forget that the wind is blowing their scent into it while traveling. We must consider where we will finally sit but absolutely must figure out a way to get to it without dragging and blowing scent into these critical areas. Take a look at these images to illustrate this point.

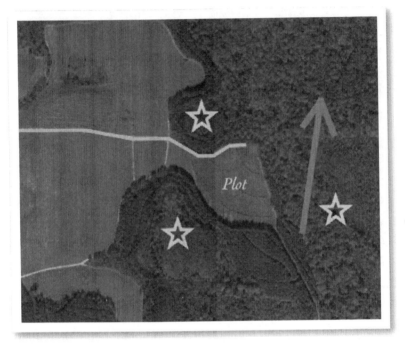

This image shows a typical Georgia setup. Imagine this is the area that you want to hunt on your farm. The arrow shows the wind direction the morning that you want to hunt. The square block is the stand you want to hunt. The deer typically travel from the areas marked with a star and come to the food source marked "Plot." While sitting in the stand, the wind blows your scent away from the food plot where you expect the deer to feed. That's certainly a good thing. You would not sit in this stand if the wind were blowing in a southern direction. The highlighted road marks the easiest way to the stand. What I want to call attention to is this: If you take that route to the stand, there is a problem that many people overlook.

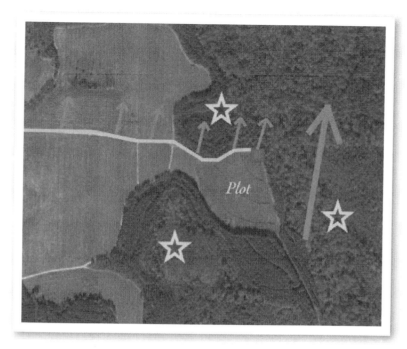

Image 2 shows your scent that will be dispersed during your walk to the stand. In this example, one of your key areas holding deer is potentially affected by the wind crossing your walking path. This may reduce your chances of seeing a mature deer from this location. Furthermore, if you get winded or seen walking in, those deer may blow, spook, and run into another area, alerting the other deer within earshot of the danger.

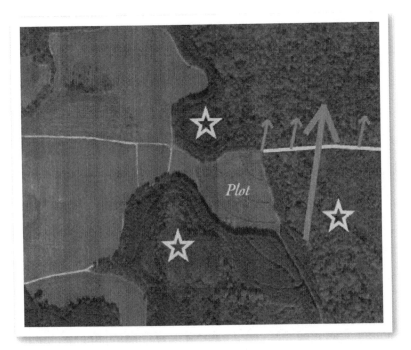

Image 3 shows a better route to the stand that doesn't allow your scent to blow into the area where you expect the deer to be, and where you think they will come from after sunrise. This is a plowed firebreak that is accessible from another location on the farm. This route is a better choice, given what you know about prior deer patterns and the current wind direction.

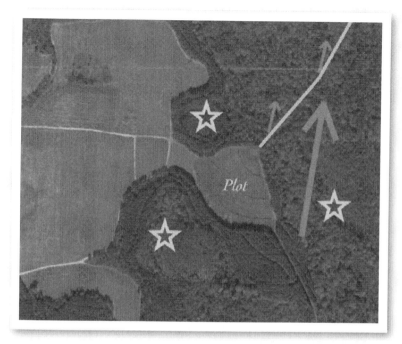

Image 4 shows an ideal route to the stand, assuming that a quiet option is available to get there. Maybe it's a dry creek bed, an old logging road, or an easy route through pine rows. If it's an available route, considering the current wind variables, this is the best option for travel to and from this particular stand location. The scent dispersion on the walk to the stand and during the hunt is minimized on this route because you are walking more directly into the wind, reducing the scent dispersion into a smaller area. In other words, you are giving up less contaminated territory and reducing your risks. This approach shrinks the area that your scent covers and won't tip the deer off that are bedding before their afternoon feed.

You catch my drift here (pun intended). We must consider where to sit and also, how to get there. Always think of multiple places to sit and multiple options on how to get there.

I know that a lot of successful hunters will prefer to drive someone to the stand in the truck and drop them off, rather than walking a long way. This reduces the human scent but obviously, adds noise. Noise is not as critical as scent control, so, in many cases, I support this strategy. I think that if the deer hear a truck, and this is a place where trucks typically drive, it's OK. In contrast, if they smell you, it's a deal breaker no matter where you are. The noise is the lesser of two evils if you can't make a quiet walk. I would rather eliminate both. If you hunt a big area that doesn't have much vehicle traffic and is usually quiet, the truck noise could tip off the deer to your presence. Electric golf carts are even better to get someone in and out of the stand because of the quiet motor. I'm not a big fan of loud 4-wheelers and gas-powered ATV's for use in the hunting areas. I prefer to walk a long way on a normally quiet farm.

I have also routinely used a mountain bike to get in and out of places that needed to be quiet, but I had long roads to travel. You laugh, but it's worked many times for me. A bicycle is a lot easier to hide than a truck, ATV, or golf cart too. It gets you there quietly, quickly, and leaves very little sign behind. I don't know anyone else that uses this method, but it has worked for me in many situations.

After seeing this buck show up on the trail camera consistently in the late mornings, I had to wait four weeks for the correct wind to hunt him in the spot he was frequently visiting. A southwest wind finally showed up on a day that I had told my 7-year-old son we could hunt together. We capitalized on the rare and unique wind opportunity and closed the deal. Resisting the urge to hunt the right buck in the wrong conditions pays off.

ATTRACTANTS

I need to say just a few words on attractants. I am talking about scent attractants — not minerals, supplements, calls, or edible treats. There is an entire aisle dedicated to this stuff in most hunting stores. It's enough to make a hunter dizzy and confused. Scent dripping devices, drags, sprays, pads, hangers, stickers, bombs, and bottles are everywhere. As I mentioned earlier, I prefer to smell like nothing. If I am planning to use a deer scent, I try to use a fresh, real scent gland from a local deer. Some of you still want to try out some of these other gadgets and lures, and that's fine. Please let me know if you find something that works **repeatedly** and **never** causes any deer to spook or become nervous. I have had some attractants seem to work for me on a few occasions, but I have also used some that definitively ruined a hunt. I must reiterate the aforementioned point that preventing mistakes is the goal. Remember, we are trying to eliminate failure, not create magic.

The main point that I want you to consider about these items is that whatever you use, think about how you are going to place it. What I mean is that if you have to walk all over your food plot dragging a urine soaked rag on a string, you just also drug human odor all over it too. You are walking, breathing, and rubbing against the foliage. There is a risk associated with putting out scents in your otherwise undisturbed honey hole. There is noise and also human scent to consider. If you are doing it in the morning before sunrise, the noise and extended flashlight use may foil your plan. Walking to multiple spots down each of your shooting lanes to hang a wick could ruin your hunt. Whatever you do, minimize your time there. Hunters also have to think about removing the scent delivery items after the hunt.

The delivery method is a critical decision in the overall scent game plan. The other choice to make is which scents to purchase. A general rule on buying scents is that you should match the scent to the situation so that things seem the most natural. We should not use a musky buck bomb or a standing estrous scent unless the deer are in active rut. If the deer are not in rut, these scents don't make sense. A doe-in-heat scent during early bow season in Georgia is a mistake. I would also stay away from scents that have additional foreign smells like apples or cinnamon. If you have been feeding apples and cinnamon in that spot all year, then maybe that's OK. Just strive to make the scent seem natural to the local environment. Radishes and honey don't grow on white oak trees in Georgia swamps. Big bucks are smart. Respect that. Again, we want them to keep doing their normal routine and remain oblivious to us ever being there.

I mentioned it before, and I will remind you again. Having real live deer in your food plot is far superior to anything that you could buy, spray, and scatter in the woods. The only way to keep happy, live decoys is to prevent mistakes that would alert deer of your presence.

CHAPTER 4
Taking a Stand

STAND FUNDAMENTALS

Where to place a stand is, of course, super-critical. We will talk about hunting from the ground later. Right now, let's focus on tree stands. We will hit on box stands and blinds in a bit too. Learning the right way to hang a stand, where to place it, and which direction to face the seat are all things that take practice (and likely some failure) to tweak just right. Finding the perfect method will come from experience. For now, let's just talk about definite mistakes to avoid and a few mandatory steps to practice every time.

Don't forget to brush it in. The stand must be hidden. If you can send a new hunting buddy into your property to sit on one of your stands for an afternoon hunt, and you don't need to escort him there and help him find it, it's probably in a location that is too open and obvious. If it's a ladder, leave some natural cover in front of both the ladder and the seat. If it's a lock-on with a removable ladder, use the tree trunk to hide the ladder and again, keep cover in front of both the ladder and the seat. When hunting from a climber, stop climbing at a spot that has plenty of cover. Don't assume that being in the clouds on a bare tree will save you. Always have cover. This is critical for the paranoid deer that we hunt in our state. If you get spotted by a deer while sitting in the stand in Georgia, you are in trouble because they will react to you in some way. If it's a mature deer, you're probably toast. In Kansas, you can often sit on a telephone pole in an open field, and the deer may never look up. In Illinois, they will sometimes look directly at you and then return right back to feeding. They might even see you move, run off alerted, then return in 20 minutes. But in the Peach State, it's an entirely different ballgame, my friend. You can be completely motionless and surrounded by cover, but if that buck looks up at you and senses that something is off, he's out of there in a flash. He will likely not return that entire day and may not even return for the entire season. We must blend in at all times. You may only get a few chances to have perfect timing for Mr. Big. Don't blow it by being visible to him. Your buddy who has never been to the stand should be able to walk right by it and never see it. If it can be seen from afar, reconsider the placement. Human vision is inferior to that of your dream buck. It's not just the buck you have to watch out for on this topic either. A paranoid mother doe and her gang of other attentive moms will be persistently scanning for any signs of disarray. She will likely be the first one to the spot. If you don't manage to fool her and she leaves upset, you have a much lower chance of seeing him. Mature bucks will often rely on does to scout an area before they enter into it. It should also be noted that in the early season when fawns are in tow, does will be on an even more heightened alert than other times of the year.

1. **Attempting to achieve 360-degree views and wide-open shots in every direction is risky.** A very common mistake that hunters make is getting saw happy. They will trim back and remove every vine, limb, and tree within 5 feet of their ladder, climb up into the stands, and then cut down everything that their 14-foot pole saw will reach. I get it; you want to be able to see everything. I wish that were possible without compromising stealth, but it's not. You want clear shots. I get it. I do too. The problem is that there will be no shot opportunity on Big Bubba Buck if you do this. Let being hidden be priority number one. With bow hunting, it's exponentially more important because you have to move so much more to draw your bow, and, on top of that, he must be very close to you. We must give up some vision and potential shooting windows to gain adequate concealment. Most likely, the buck is not going to walk the line that you anticipate he will walk. It just doesn't work that way most of the time. He's probably not going to stop in the shooting lane you

created, or set up in the middle of your food plot. Whatever he does, he's not likely going to do the same thing twice. Allow yourself a few opportunities in a few directions, but know that you cannot write the script and that if you get greedy with where you want to see, you will be seen. It's insanely frustrating and heartbreaking to have a trophy deer at 35 yards, bow in hand, with no shot. It's also exhilarating and a lot of fun though. In contrast, never seeing him at all is depressing. As long as you don't make a catastrophic mistake, you may get another chance. If he can see you from 120 yards (and be certain that he is looking from there), you will never get him to 35. I know it stinks, but, once again, patience and discipline are a must here. Being completely concealed and only having a few shot options is a better bet than being visible and having bigger shot windows.

2. **Create or find a way to get into the spot without creating a raucous.** More specifically, you must be able to get to, into, and out of the stand, without making any noise. If you find a honey hole, but you have to walk through 400 yards of 6-inch-deep dry oak leaves to get there, you likely need to reconsider. Every deer within a quarter of a mile can hear your 8-minute-long, deafening trek. On a quiet morning, this is like sounding a warning gong. That may be the spot for a morning with heavy dew on the ground or one that is reserved for post-rainy weather when the leaves can be trampled without crunching.

Place stands in locations where you can slip in and out easily and undetected. Deer will spook based on the way you walk and what they hear. They don't necessarily even have to see you or smell you. If you have been hunting a while, you can probably now listen from the tree and definitively know the difference between the footsteps of a squirrel, an armadillo, a coyote, a chasing buck, a feeding deer, or an alert deer. This is all from mere human listening. With a better set of ears and a more attentive and paranoid attitude, I assure you that deer know when an intruder is walking around. That is unless they can't hear it at all. If you have a small harrow and tractor, keep firebreaks and trails tilled. This makes for easy, quiet travel and also provides a great canvas for scouting footprints, which help with learning size, number, and travel direction of deer too. Sometimes a good spot may have one short and easy, but noisy, way in, or a longer, harder route that is better for sound and wind. Choose the longer, quieter route, and you will be better off. I also think it's critical to change travel plans based on current conditions.

3. **You don't have to be on the hotspot every time.** Sometimes it's better to be on the deer's route to or from the hotspot than camping out right on the bullseye. The natural tendency is to want to be right on the spot where the most sign is. That may be a sure-fire way to get busted. Place the stand in view of the spot,

but at the further limits of your shot range. Another option is to be close to the main trails and ambush them on their way to and from the feeding spot, even if you can't see the actual gathering area. Deer are usually more alert in open areas and high-traffic locations. You are not the only predator they are watching out for. Set stands a few trees back off the food plot or trail, instead of right on it. If you know your shooting capabilities and practice regularly (we'll talk more about that later), you know what shots you can make, and need to back up and trust your skills. Another problem with being too close is that if a group of deer comes at the same time, you may not be able to draw the bow or raise the gun because their eyes are all around you. Having the freedom to study from a distance is very valuable. Think like a sniper.

STAND SELECTION

Should I use a ladder stand, a hang-on type stand, or a climber? As long as you are physically able and practiced at each, you should have all of these in your arsenal for when you need them. Ladder stands are the safest and easiest to use. They have been around forever. I grew up hunting in 8-foot-tall, one piece, homemade ladder stands. I now know that being higher than 8 feet off the ground is way more advantageous, but in my hometown, 8 to 10 feet was the standard for a long time. Now, there are some light, sectional ladder stands that are easy to set up and will allow you to sit at 12, 15, or 18 feet. Sometimes it takes two people to set them up, depending on weight and height. The only problem is that the ladder is usually pretty obvious to the people and the animals in the area.

Hang-on or lock-on type stands allow you to be more concealed, but are also more dangerous to get into and out of. They can be trickier to set up too, even with the handy tools and devices available. Most accidents occur during the tricky transition when moving from the last step of the ladder onto the stand platform, or when moving back onto the ladder from the stand platform. Some people hang removable ladder sections by strapping them onto the tree. Others screw or nail in pegs that are used as steps. Stick ladders that come in sections are very popular and convenient as well. All of these are pretty easy to travel with because they break down, stack together, and fold up. They allow you to get into most any type of tree and place the height wherever you think you need it. These stands can be brushed-in and hidden well. If you aren't very agile or coordinated, don't use these stands. If you do use these, you should absolutely wear a harness and be able to attach the safety tether strap during the critical transition from ladder to stand and back. There are some well-designed safety systems for these stands. The safest ones keep you tethered during the entire climb and also during the critical transitions in and out.

Before I forget, I need to remind you about other minute details that could ruin a hunt. The C-clips that are used to piece ladder sections together are sometimes a major noise problem. Consider replacing these with a nut and bolt instead of an attachment that can move, rattle, or get kicked. If you use the clips, have the movable part on the back side of the ladder, not the front. This prevents them from being bumped while climbing. The rubber coated ones are best. Remember, there is no natural sound in the woods that sounds like metal parts banging together.

What about climbers? Climbers provide a portable, sometimes backpack-style solution. Climbers are great for sitting in a new area to learn patterns before mounting a time-consuming setup and trimming lanes, etc. They require some skill to use but are not too difficult. The downside is that climbing a tree can be noisy. If you use them, practice doing it slowly and quietly. Another setback is that you have to have a relatively straight tree with no limbs from the ground up to where you want to sit. In Georgia, luckily there usually isn't a shortage of good pine trees.

Use your discretion on what stands to use but remember, it needs to be safe, hidden, and quiet. You also have to decide whether to leave the climber at the base of the tree or take it with you. If you can install, uninstall, and move quietly, I say take it with you. Leaving it to be discovered by roaming deer may be detrimental to your success in that spot. If you can't handle installation and removal quietly and quickly, it may be better to leave it on the tree instead of adding more noise on the day of the hunt. Either way, spray it down with scent eliminator before you take it into the timber. If you leave it, do your best to hide it. Do not place it directly on a well-traveled trail.

How high should I sit? We know that deer see a little differently than humans. They have more of a panoramic view of their surroundings than we do. They can see almost 300 degrees horizontally and only have about a 60-degree blind spot behind them. This wide-angle view is clear and allows them to pick up movement on the horizon. This clear zone is wide, but not very tall. In other words, if your big buck is scanning the brush at eye level, he is not able to see things that are too high off the ground clearly without raising his head and gazing upwards. This is an unnatural movement and an uncommon tendency for deer because predators (other than you) are typically at ground level. Usually, deer will not look up unless they are already alert or suspicious. For this reason, being higher is certainly advantageous. The height you choose is a matter of convenience, cover, safety, and physical ability. I usually buy ladder stands from 12 to 15 feet tall. I hang my lock-ons from 15-20, and I rarely ascend above 20, even in a climber. If you are rifle hunting, you can effectively hunt higher than with a bow, but there is more risk of severe personal injury if you were to fall out. Beware of perching too high when bow hunting because it does affect the shot. If you hunt at 18 feet with a bow, you need to practice from there too. The angle and the drop matter, but perhaps the most important thing with the bow is the time between when the bowstring pops and the arrow connects. The sound can make a buck move several inches very quickly, and those few inches could be the difference in a clean kill and a non-lethal or non-trackable wound. Sit where you are comfortable, where you can see, and where you can be covered well. Don't forget to be quiet. If your stand squeaks, creaks, or rattles, fix it. Lube it, wrap it, tighten it, and replace squeaky parts.

Regardless of where you set the stands, once they are set, resist the urge to go in there and look around for deer sign. Every trip to the stand reduces your chance of killing a dream buck. The very first time you sit in there, which may be the first time you ever go in there, will be the best opportunity. Don't put cameras and feed right around the stand if they require maintenance and multiple trips in. I reiterate, every human exposure reduces your chances of killing a big, smart, bruiser buck. If he detects your presence, he will use the area more cautiously or will abandon it.

What about box stands, shooting houses, and ground blinds? Big stands with multiple seats and plenty of legroom are great for taking kids, camera gear, and staying out of the wind and weather. It's good to have a few stands with a roof for those days when heavy rain is likely. In the great state of Georgia, I don't think temporary, removable ground blinds produce great results unless you leave them out there for a while. Tower stands and shooting houses are good to have on the farm, especially in big fields and food plots. The key to these big stands is that they need to be out there a long time before you hunt out of them. It's best if they can stay in place all year. The animals need to get accustomed to these things being in the area. They will adapt. However, I have been in many of these stands, downwind of deer, and as soon as they enter the field, they look right at it and stare. Make no mistake about it; the deer will learn that these are often occupied by hunters and behave accordingly.

If you have good food and the right wind, you should expect to see deer on these stands, but you will likely have more success with big bucks in a more secretive setup. The exception to that generalization would come during the rut and post-rut. Usually, early season on big food plots isn't your best tactic to find a bruiser. If you pop up your doghouse blind and expect to get a giant buck to walk within bow range an hour later, you are just wishful thinking. This would be a rare event in our state. You see it work flawlessly sometimes on TV. At least, that is what we are to believe. I'm not going to discourage the use of big stands. Just leave them out there and remember to have a few, more intimate setups deep in the timber too. If you use box stands or other stands with a shooting rail, wrap the rails with something soft, like a foam pipe insulator, to cut down on noise when you prop up your gun, binoculars, or rangefinder on the rail. Instead of having open windows on each side of the stand, try to black out the back windows and only monitor one or two directions. If there is no window or light behind you, you are less likely to get busted because you stay in the shadows and your silhouette cannot be identified. It's a useful practice to place someone in your stand and observe what they look like sitting there from multiple vantage points, particularly from where the deer will be.

Another valuable stand tactic to consider is something that many people never use. That is, having multiple stands in the same areas so that you have different options for different conditions. It costs more to have multiple stands in the same area, but having an option on opposite ends of a good hunting spot can be very advantageous. We already established that bad wind is a deal breaker. We cannot sit in a stand that enables the wind to blow our scent to the deer. So if you have a stand on multiple sides of the food plot or trail, you can decide which ambush point to use. I have observed something very useful and interesting on multiple occasions. That is, when sitting in a new, additional stand on an old spot, the deer will often observe and study the other, older stand before stepping into the area. In other words, I have watched deer carefully analyze the empty stand because they know it's there. This is especially true if you have been spotted in a stand before. Mix it up.

One more tip is to be creative. I have hunted from farm equipment, abandoned houses, and even trash piles. If the structure has been there for a long time and the deer don't mind it, use it if you can. Sometimes that's better than adding something new to the landscape. Just be careful and check for other critters that may use the same sites for their home.

CHAPTER 5
Travel Plans

We talked about where to put the stand, but there are also a few additional items to discuss regarding how to get to the location you plan to hunt. I already touched on noise and scent issues to consider when traveling to and from stands. I want to expand on those and a few more items.

What about flashlights? Are deer scared of them? If you were to survey a group of hunters, many would say no, most would say yes, and others would say it doesn't change their game plan either way. I would like to impose on you the idea that flashlights most certainly spook deer. There are strategic ways to use them if you need them. Let's simply agree to use them sparingly and in a way that improves our chances of remaining undetected. We can never be too careful or too stealthy.

One of my pet peeves is the haphazard way that

some sportsmen use reflective trail markers. Some hunters put reflective tacks on trees, others use clips, and some use stakes or poles. These things are not a bad idea in and of themselves, but they should not be used flippantly. No matter which one you use, if you use any, place them as low as possible, and use as few as possible to get the job done. If your clip is on a limb 8 feet above the ground, where must you shine to see it? UP! If your tacks are eye level, you have to constantly pan with your light at that level. When the farm is dark, light travels a long way. Waving your 700 lumen light back and forth on the trail assures that any deer within two miles will be glaring at it. If the markers are lower, and you never raise your light above ground level, naturally, less light is scattered, and you are much better off. Another good tip is to keep the placement consistent. If you are traveling down a trail, put all the markers on the same side of the travel path, so you get into a rhythm of where to look and don't have to shine your light back and forth so much. Place them at the same height on every tree and space them at equal step intervals. This way, you know where and when to expect to see one and don't have to search. This method will also cut down on you lighting up the entire farm on the way in and out.

When using a light, you need to have a few different types. I have a "getting dressed at the truck" light, a "walking" light, and a "tracking" light. The one for the truck is a moderately bright, wide range, headlamp. This is an all-purpose light and can be used for tracking and dragging too. The one I like to walk with is very low power and has a red lens. Deer seem to be less spooked by red, and you can confirm this when coyote hunting with a red lens and deer are in the area too. This light should be used when walking to and from the stand, and kept pointed down. The super-duper, crazy-bright, retina burner is only for finding wounded and dead deer. Simple enough right?

We talked about sound a little bit, and I mentioned how you could distinguish the gait of different animals just by listening to the rustle of the leaves. This idea leads to a noteworthy issue that most everyone ignores. The following trick is a game-changer that very few people use and a super simple one to implement. When in the woods, hunters need to walk differently than they do in everyday life. I know some of you think this is overkill, but hear me out. If your trip to the stand isn't likely to be totally quiet, and some walking sound is imminent, then why not sound like something other than a hunter? No animals in the woods walk at a consistent, upright, two-legged, unbroken gate, for six minutes, with equal foot placement on every step. I also know that no animal in the Georgia woods wears two size 12 boots either. We make a character-istic, rhythmic, heavy sound when we walk around. We should try to sound like something other than a person walking. Deer don't mind the sound of a squirrel, a turkey, or an armadillo. So how do you sound like something other than the buck-crazed maniac that you are? You change your stride and alter the speed. You sound less alarming if you occasionally stop with a different length of pause each time you take a step. You won't believe how many more deer you will hear and see by stopping, listening, and looking too. There are so many times when deer are watching you walk by, and you never know it. Does will usually take off once they see you, but bucks will often remain completely still and just let you pass. We will cover still-hunting and a ground game later. This type of patient walking will be even more critical to be successful at stalking deer. When you do stop walking and begin to listen, you will often realize that there are animals very close by. If they haven't seen you or your light yet, they may not blast out of there. They might just keep feeding and milling around. I have stopped many times before getting to my stand, realizing that the deer are between me and my destination. I will crouch down or sit against a tree and allow the sun to rise instead of bumping the animals and scaring them off trying to get into my stand. I have killed quite a few using this approach, never even making it to the stand. These pauses are good for breaking your sound up, and also for allowing you to hear what's going on around you.

You may laugh, but if I am going through a thick bottom, sometimes I will shuffle in there slowly to sound more like a rooting hog or an armadillo. I will quickly run a few steps here and there to sound more like a squirrel or small quick animal. I killed a big buck during peak rut once by skipping like an elementary school girl and sounding like a chasing pair of galloping deer in the dry leaves. Two bucks strutted right into the dry creek bottom on one of my pauses after hearing me do it. Hey, it worked. I don't recommend that move. It just happened to be a special time when I knew the bucks were love crazy and chasing does, and

I thought it was worth a try. Sometimes you have to think outside of the box. People wearing boots crush leaves and twigs when they walk. Nothing else in the Georgia woods does that like we do. Pay attention to your steps. Pick soft spots without foliage to walk on. Every step matters. Keep your trails as clean as possible. Whatever it takes to be quiet is going to be the best. Total silence is preferred. However, there is no way around it, and you must make noise, change it up a little and don't just have one, unbroken, consistent stride all the way to the stand. In areas with heavy turkey activity, stopping to cluck with your turkey call may even help a listening deer to relax.

How you creep to the stand is very important, but how you leave is too. After your hunt, don't disregard all these things, blow them off, and blast out of there. Don't make a phone call, take a leak, and haphazardly walk back to the truck. Often, the deer are close by after the hunt, and it's important to keep them happy and not give them any extra clues to use against you next time. Being undetected after the hunt is just as critical as it is when you arrive. Remember, we don't want them to change patterns. We want them to keep doing what they do, and eventually, we learn how to adapt and execute a plan around them.

CHAPTER 6
Ground Game

Hunting from the ground is a lost art. It can be very effective, and it's free! There are many cool stands at the hunting store, and a lot of them are quite comfortable. Stands are beneficial in many settings. For many people, sitting in a tree just feels more legit for a deer hunt. Most people don't ever consider sitting directly on the ground. I am here to tell you that you need to consider it, especially if you are a gun hunter. I don't know how many deer I have successfully taken over my hunting career, but I can claim with certainty that at least 40% of them have been harvested from the ground. Yep, 40%! I have been accused of having ADHD and being incapable of sitting still in a tree, but I have also sat in uncomfortable tree stands from sun up to sun down when I thought it was prudent to do so.

We will cover still-hunting, stalking, and moving

around on the ground in a later chapter. For now, let's just focus on finding a good spot and staying there for the entire hunt. Even if you love tree stands, towers, and blinds, you need to have a ground game in your strategic plan. In time, it will likely become a big part of your hunting portfolio as you get more experienced. This option is always open for me. Sometimes it's the only option and very often, the preferred choice. Let me give you four reasons why ground hunting is advantageous.

1. Convenience – To find bucks, scouting is necessary. We know this. However, tracks, rubs, scrapes, and pictures only tell you parts of the story. To study the area and the animals in it, you have to sit there and observe. You will learn the deer's preferences, tendencies, and travel patterns for the area. Sometimes you spend two hours lugging in ladders, straps, stands and getting them set. Then you spend another two hours trimming limbs, arranging cover, and creating shooting lanes. When you finally get a chance to sit there a few weeks later after meticulously modifying the habitat and dragging scent around, you realize that you need to be 60 yards further down the trail, or that the spot isn't a good one at all. Now you have to do it all over again. Setting up another spot takes time and even worse, increases the chances that you will disturb the habitat and influence the deer to change what they naturally want to do. If your first few sits were on the ground, you could adjust easily without any extra work. Your first sit in a new stand is usually the best one. But your first trip into the spot is exponentially better than that. What I mean is that if your first time into a new bottom is the hunt itself, you will have much better chances of seeing your monster because he has no prior clues of your presence. If it's an afternoon hunt, you can get there a few minutes early for an easy setup. If it's a morning hunt before daylight, just get close to where you need to be, sit down anywhere, and wait for sunrise to fine-tune your spot. Just know that you can stealthily move a little bit once the sun starts to come up if you don't like the spot. When there is no prior damage, no equipment that the deer have seen, and no lingering scent, you will be amazed at how effective this method is.

2. Unlimited options – Sometimes, in a prime spot, there is not a favorable tree for your stand. If you are hunting with a climber, only specific trees work. If you are in lock-on, sometimes you can't see from a high vantage point and sometimes there isn't enough cover to hide you. If you prefer a ladder, there may not be a way to hide it, and you may have to cut 40 limbs to make it fit. But, if you are a ground guy, you can sit almost anywhere, and you are not depending on an ideal tree to have grown in the ideal spot. You can sit in a bush or a bunch of brush in a folding chair, or lean against any tree and sit on the ground. Sitting against a big tree trunk is usually best for blending and to conceal movement. You just need a few limbs, sticks, or grass patches around you for added cover. It's easy to quickly gather and assemble some cover if there isn't an ideal setup already there. Just remember that you don't need to erect a fortress. A few natural items in front of you to help break up your silhouette will do the trick. Having ground sitting options means you can hunt almost anywhere. In many areas, you have much more visibility from the ground than you do being in a tree. Just be sure that the wind is right . . . Always!

3. Keeping them guessing - Another benefit to hunting from the ground is the ability to change the spot from one hunt to the next. Think about it. If you sit in the same spot for four hours, then do it a few times over a month, your chances of tipping the deer off increases. Returning to the scene of the crime is a way to get busted. If you mix it up and hunt the same area, but from a different spot each time, they cannot pinpoint a specific spot to avoid. I assure you that the deer in a given area do learn your spots over time. I have moved 50-100 yards from a previous spot and watched deer come into an area to stage and scope out the previous spot. They will stand at a safe and hidden distance for a long time, looking right at the exact tree where I sat before to see if anything is fishy. They must have smelled me after I left the location on a prior trip.

4. Stealth - Walking to a tree stand and walking to a ground spot will have the same risk of being seen, heard, or smelled. However, if you are not having to climb and move yourself and your gear into a stand once you get there, you can cut out a lot of the extra risks of being detected. It's a lot easier to see a 180-pound object in the woods if it's 6, 8, 10, or 15 feet off the ground and moving. Climbing puts you in a vulnerable spot to be seen. It also usually adds foreign noises that are unnatural to the woods. Ladders squeak, stretch, and creak. Clips get bumped and dinged. Pulling your gear up by a rope and it getting snagged or rubbed makes noise. When you are wearing six layers of clothing and have limited coordination and mobility, you inevitably bang your gun on the rail or your bow on the ladder. Almost all climbers make some noise. Some stands sound like a chainsaw when moving up a tree. Accidentally dropping some of your gear can sound like a car crash in the wee hours of the morning. There is no way to know how many times a big buck hears the commotion and quietly slips away, but you can bet that it happens. Easing in and sitting down quickly and quietly will reduce the chances of being busted.

If you are going to hunt on the ground, safety is a concern and should be treated with utmost respect. Bullets travel a long way, and we need to make sure that you aren't firing them into an unintended location. Ground sitting can also increase your chances of being accidentally shot. It's critical to know where all other hunters are positioned. Although not required by law, I also recommend wearing some orange on your head, not just your torso. It's imperative to know the property, the boundaries, who else is on the farm, and also your shooting ballistics. Hunters should never shoot in a way that allows the bullet to reach an unsafe area. I hope this is common sense, but ground shooting requires more knowledge and consideration to be safe. Never assume that you are alone. Stay visible to other hunters. Do not take unclear shots. Think safety.

This 11-point was harvested from the ground on the first trip into a previously undisturbed area. No one had been in this section of the property in years. I had not been in there to hang a stand, to set up a camera, or to feed. I quietly walked in one afternoon when the wind was favorable, found a small opening with a heavy trafficked trail, and sat on the ground. I saw three bucks during that hunt and shot this one from my homemade ground blind. I had pictures of the same buck in a different location a month earlier, but he had disappeared since then.

CHAPTER 7
Blending In

What about camouflage patterns? Is one clothing pattern any more successful than the others? I have seen old timers that still use faded out army camo very successfully. You know, the ambiguous shape patterns of Kelly green, brown, and black without any leaves, tree bark, or sticks? I know some guys that don't wear camo at all, they just forge on in jeans and an everyday jacket. Most modern hunters have photo quality, realistic images on their clothes. One new trend is using digital camo patterns generated from mathematical equations. There is no need to fight about this subject. You can probably kill a deer in a hot pink tutu if you can sit still enough, stay downwind, and pick the right time and hunting spot. However, let's just take a common-sense approach and say that wearing a pattern that looks mostly identical to the environment where you are sitting is probably the most logical plan. The realistic looking patterns are easy to find and affordable. The common mistake that many hunters make is not the clothing; it's where they sit in that clothing and how they move around. We can't go wrong looking exactly like the area where we are sitting.

Understanding silhouettes is important. From a distance, your hunting jacket that looks just like a tree can look totally different. At 90 yards, you may look like a big solid brown blob. This is especially true of older, faded clothing. There are not too many 6-foot tall, man-shaped, monotone things that live in the woods of Georgia and climb trees. This image is likely to spook a deer or at least tip them off to the fact that it (you) is not normal. To blend better and remain hidden, we need to break up that image. The best way to do this is with shadows and with natural cover. When you are in a tree stand, it's super-valuable to have some branches between you and the deer's eyes. As we laid out in a prior chapter, don't underestimate the need to keep some cover around you. Some guys will go nuts with their pruners and pole saw, hacking everything so that they have a clear field of view and a wide-open shot opportunity in every direction. This is a mistake. It's a massive mistake for bow hunters that need deer within close range. A mature buck will not parade under you at 20 yards if he sees a 212-pound blob on top of a clean ladder. Keep as much cover as possible. If no natural cover is available, make some. Move branches and stack them or hang them to help conceal your body. I have taken the power screwdriver up and screwed branches onto trees where no other native cover was present. If you do this, be sure to use coated, non-reflective screws.

We must also consider sunlight and where the sun rises and sets. If the area where the deer are active has a lot of shade, but your stand is in direct sunlight, you can be seen from a long way away. It's vitally important to be under some cover. Having a bunch of limbs and leaves above you is an asset when it comes to light and shade. Irregular shadows and broken, inconsistent light beams are assets. We can use this phenomenon of light and shadows to our advantage to supplement our concealment efforts. Irregular shadows and broken light beams are an asset. Even after the leaves fall, if there are sticks and limbs that cast many shade lines over you, you can virtually disappear. Of course, as the sun rises and sets, these angles change constantly. If you know the general line where the sun moves, you can be sure that there is cover for any time of the hunt. A full shadow is beneficial, but a broken up, inconsistent one is even better. Sit behind some cover and also under some cover. Make sure that your entire body is never in full sunlight. I recommend wearing a hat with a bill for shading your eyes, and a head net/ face cover too.

CHAPTER 8
Sitting Lessons

Now we've erected a stand in the right spot. We snuck in quietly and undetected. We are as scent-free as possible and have the wind in our favor. A large part of the work is done. Now what? Now we wait. Make no mistake, even if everything else is perfectly executed, the successful hunters are killing deer after deer because they are putting in the time. How long we wait certainly matters, but beyond the time, exactly how we wait will prove to be another significant factor that determines whether or not we drag a 200-pound beast out of the woods. Again, remember our rationale. We need to prevent critical errors while maximizing the number of viable opportunities.

It's really easy to be excited and overactive in the stand, especially in a good spot. Stands, where action can and will happen all around you and in every direction, can be really fun or can be very frustrating. Sometimes it's better to sit in a tight spot where there are only one or two shooting lanes or areas to watch. This prevents us from needing to look around so much, constantly turning and shifting in the stand. Is there a right way to survey the hunting grounds from the stand? You bet! We need to set up the stand so that the main area to watch is available to see from a comfortable position that requires little effort. I mean you can sit for a long time, without moving or getting uncomfortable, and always see the key spot. You don't want to have to lean over, rise up and down, or need to turn your body 180 degrees to see deer. Furthermore, we need to be able to easily adjust to shoot with minimal effort.

Sometimes, sitting in prime spots means that there are multiple areas to monitor. If you need to look back and forth to cover many areas, you must have a plan for how to look. I know this is a small detail, but limiting the number of times that you move increases success. It's that simple. So if we need to look at four different spots every few minutes, it would be beneficial to have a system.

First off is the right way to move. Always move your eyes first, without moving your torso or even your head. Lead with your eyes, moving your head only when necessary. Stay as close to the tree as possible and maintain the same distance from the tree. When it is necessary to move your head, move only your head. Try not to move your torso and do not move your back and shoulders away from the tree. From a side profile, the head is not too different of a shape or size than the front profile. So if you are a silhouette, a head turning is hard to see, especially if it's slow. In contrast, the side and front profile of the rest of your body is very different in size and shape. We don't want to turn in a way that changes that silhouette and gives us away. Keep this in mind. Some hunters stand while bow hunting. If you need to stand, stay as close to the tree as possible and obey the same rules for eye, head, and body movement. If possible, try not to allow any space or light between you and the tree.

Be patient, don't scan everything the entire hunt. Sweep across with your eyes first, followed by your head, moving slowly and checking thoroughly and methodically. We must stop regularly and stare in one direction. Sweeping eyesight and scanning movement is not the best way to find deer in their natural habitat. A fixed position and a prolonged, deliberate stare are always more effective than sweeping, quick glances. More times than not, we are looking for one side of a single tail flicker, a dark, skinny leg, a bush slightly moving, or an ear flash. If deer didn't have white patches in multiple locations, we would hardly ever see them. To pick up on the tiny, stealthy movement, we have to focus on one area for extended periods. Learning how to patiently scan with binoculars is a valuable tool that seasoned hunters use to locate deer that novices would otherwise miss.

CHAPTER 9
Calls of the Wild

W hat about calls? The hunting store has deer calls for rattling, grunting, wheezing, bleating, and more. They are in the form of bags, tubes, shakers, cans, whistles, and who knows what else. So what are they all for and when do you use them?

Rattling is supposed to sound like two bucks fighting, mimicking two racks banging against each other. Fighting is a natural part of a buck's life. In the early season, bucks will spar with each other playfully. They do this as a social function, to practice their skills and get stronger, and I think, just for recreational, physical play like boys do. During and around the rut, bucks will fight more aggressively, sometimes to the death. Bucks most certainly do fight each other and produce an audible noise. Hunting shows and magazine articles make us believe that it happens all the time, and that rattling works like magic to bring them in close. This is not the case, especially in Georgia. Here are the two questions that I encourage you to ask yourself before I move on.

1. How many times have you been hunting?
2. How many times have you heard bucks fighting while you were hunting?

If you are honest, the ratio is probably about 100 to 1. So then we must admit that rattling every time we enter the woods probably isn't a natural sounding occurrence to the resident whitetails. Remember, we don't want them to change behavior. We want to remain undetected and allow them to comfortably do what they naturally want to do.

I'm not saying that rattling is always a bad idea, but I think it's often a bad idea in Georgia. Well, at least it's only effective in very select situations. There is a right way to do it and a right time to try. My advice on rattling is not to use it to try to make some crazy action start to happen on a slow and otherwise quiet morning outside. Rather, use it on an awesome morning with heightened deer activity to make a good day even better. On an active day with aggressive behavior, it's at least plausible to the deer in the area that a fight could actually be happening. On an early season day when it's hot, with no rut activity, and all the deer are bedded down in the shade, they aren't going to rush in to see a fight that they know doesn't make sense. On the contrary, if you have seen multiple bucks chasing does and fighting during an action-packed morning, it's probably an advantageous time to try it out. On these days, you may even want to try it in multiple locations throughout the day. When the time is right, it can be a useful tool. You may even get multiple bucks to come check it out in multiple locations if the timing is perfect. I remember one morning when I rattled in three different bucks in three different spots. That was after I had seen two bucks chasing does in heat, and I had already witnessed a fight earlier that morning.

In other states, rattling can be much more effective. In Georgia, we must resist the urge to overdo it. Rattling should not be used as a desperation call, or a cure for boredom, but rather a strategic tool for the perfect situation. Social bucks will rattle at many points during the season, but it's a certain type of light activity. Rutting bucks will fight for dominance during a short window of time in the season, and it's an entirely different thing.

If you do choose to rattle, start with short sequences with breaks of silence in between. You must be listening and watching in case there are deer close by. If they come in and you are causing a big raucous at the top of a tree, shaking the entire structure, you are likely to get busted and ruin a valuable opportunity. A stand that has some blind material wrapped around it can be advantageous in helping to conceal the motion. You may even want to paint the antlers or smear some mud on them to hide the dried out, white color that can be visible from far away. Keep it mild for a sequence and see if anything shows up. Give it five or ten minutes before you try another mild set. Then wait another five or ten minutes before you turn it up a notch and make a more aggressive presentation.

Call me old-fashioned, but I still think a real pair of thick antlers is the best thing to rattle with. From a distance in the woods, they sound the best to me. If you have ever heard a pair of mature bucks really attack, it sounds heavy. It doesn't sound like the ting of the plastic or wooden rattle bags, nor does it sound like the bumpy plastic things that you rub together that make a weak tickling sound. It's deeper and more substantial. You can hear the heavy bang when they hit each other, and if you are close enough, even feel it. You also hear stomps, slams, slides, falls, and crashes into the surrounding foliage. Those noises are hard to safely and accurately emulate from a tree. I always stomp my feet and kick trees and brush if I am ground hunting.

There are a lot of cool looking calls with eye-catching features on the retail shelves. Many of them are conveniently compact and lightweight. Test them out if you must. If you want my opinion, I think real antlers produce the best sound quality, despite being cumbersome. Maybe the inconvenience of carrying them will force you to leave them out, which may be better anyway. Take them on peak days with higher opportunity, but leave them at home or in the truck the rest of the year. They are not magic wands that produce wild action from bedded, tired, or uninterested deer. They are calls that are meant to get an already jacked-up buck into kill range. It's just another tool to help close the deal. Remember, taking more gear makes it harder to stay out of sight and move quietly. Don't take the entire hunting aisle with you every time you enter the woods.

What about calls like bleats and grunts? Again, I must ask you this: How many times have you been hunting, and how many times have you hear a bleat or a grunt in the woods? In our state, the deer aren't very vocal. As you learn to get closer to more deer effectively, you will hear more of the language. They do communicate vocally, but not all day, every day. When they do, it's usually not very loud.

There are two main types of bleats. The sound of a fawn bleat is a distress signal that very young deer use to tell the mother, and the other does in the area, that something is wrong. Often, a fawn will bleat when trapped, lost, injured, scared, or in danger. A mature doe will often come to the rescue, even if it's not her own fawn in distress. Using a fawn distress call appeals to the maternal instincts of the does. In the early season when fawns are still staying with mother and nursing, fawn bleats can work to draw in mature does. It's not typically something that calls in big bucks directly, but he may show up because he is in a social group with the doe. So in early season, a distressed fawn bleat can work. Just don't expect Big Daddy to barrel in to see what the commotion is about. The other type of bleat is an estrous bleat. This is the sound a mature doe makes when she is searching for an adequate suitor. Sometimes a doe will make this noise to call area bucks to her when she is trying to locate a potential mate. Other times, does will call periodically during the chase, once she has positively identified the sire. It's a sort of flirty game that they play. The bucks will often respond by chasing and grunting. If they get separated momentarily, one may call the other to reconnect the chase. To an opportunistic buck, especially a dominant buck, these calls can be irresistible if used during the right time. If the big buck knows that a heated chase is happening and that a doe is ready to breed, he may show up, intending to challenge the male (or males) on the chase and try to steal the girl for himself. When she is ovulating, there is a short window of opportunity, and the bucks know it. So if all the conditions are right, an estrous bleat can be very helpful. But think about when this would be realistic. It would only be a legit noise during rut when action is high. This could make a decent hunt turn into an exceptional one, but will not likely make a dead morning in early season come alive.

What about grunts and snort calls? Let me just say first and foremost, be disciplined. New calls show up on the market every year, and the makers pay big bucks for TV shows and hunting celebs to tout them. Grunts can be helpful in a few rare occasions in Georgia, but don't overdo it. A male deer grunts to communicate with other deer. That is a fact. The majority of the time that you hear a buck grunting in Georgia is when he is actively on the trail of a hot doe. Sometimes they will stop and send out a few deep grunts to locate her if he can't find her. More often, they will grunt while actively trotting and running her down. Sometimes he will grunt on every bound, and it sounds awesome. One other occasion when a buck grunts is when he is challenging another buck. Sometimes they will grunt to warn other bucks that a fight may be coming if they hang around. So if a mature buck is in the area and he hears grunts, he may want to check it out to see if there is a doe in heat that is causing the buck to get excited or testy. Again, he would gladly steal the doe and capitalize on the short window of sexual opportunity that he so desires. So just like all the rest of the calls (you should be seeing a pattern by now), use them sparingly. Make it sound legit. Use grunts on days when deer are grunting or when the action warrants it. Bucks are probably not grunting, fighting, or chasing does during the first week of bow season when the deer are still in velvet.

The new things that I see on the shelves and touted on the hunting shows are the snort wheeze calls. A snort wheeze is the noise that angry, alpha male bucks make when they are announcing their prowess and are committed to a serious fight. I have seen deer perform these rare sounds on TV a few times, and seen paid hunters promote the calls often. Personally, I have only witnessed local bucks perform this unique noisy combo four times in my entire hunting career. To me, that confirms that it's pretty rare in the Georgia timber. I have witnessed many bucks in a standoff, a sparring match, and even in knock-down, drag-out fights when they are trying to kill each other. Even in those extreme cases, the bucks are not very audible. Our local bucks just don't talk all that much. When they do, it's usually soft grunts in a short period during the rut. Use your best judgment on these calls. You can see by now that my attitude remains constant with all calls. That is, less is usually more. It's probably way more important for you to locate your target, find the best way to sneak in, and then patiently wait for him to make a mistake than it is to worry about trying to call him to you. I am fully aware that this may be a buzzkill, but it would be a major disservice to you by not being honest about these issues.

CHAPTER 10
The Rut

For many, Christmas is the most wonderful time of the year. However, for the hardcore hunter, it doesn't compare to the magical season known as "the rut." This is a short, euphoric time, where awesome opportunities arise that absolutely do not exist during the rest of the year. Bucks become way more active and less attentive. They cover more ground than any other time of the year and make more mistakes. It's the best time to take a trophy from the hunting camp, hands down. If you do not hunt any other time of the year, you must show up for the rut. Be prepared to hunt often, and to sit longer than usual. During the rut, incredible opportunities can appear at any hour of the day.

People get confused about the rut, about what it is, when it is, and why it happens. Simply put, the rut is when mature does are fertile and ready to mate.

The females begin to ovulate and prepare to breed with a healthy buck. They emit unique smells, pheromones, and other signals that let the bucks know that the time is near. These "hot does" seek out a worthy sperm donor to become pregnant. The bucks are eager to capitalize on the sexual opportunity. They are willing to travel far and wide, way outside of their normal home zone, to practice their favorite activity. They are also super competitive about it. Bucks will try to reserve territory, stake claim to an area and the does within it, and will often fight if challenged. They will frequently return to monitor the does in the area in search of one that is ready to breed. Typically, the bucks move quickly and cover more ground than normal, which certainly increases the chances of him coming by you. It's common for them to lose up to 50 pounds during the rut because they run so much, looking for love, and don't even take time to eat and replenish the burned calories. A buck uses his sense of smell to know when a doe is almost ready to mate. He covers acre after acre, trying to pick up the right scent. Once he finds a doe that smells right, he will devote all of his attention to finding her. He, and a few other opportunistic bucks, will usually stay close to her so that once she is ready, he is the lucky one she chooses. In this time of intoxicated love, he will ignore his finely tuned survival skills and make foolish mistakes (not unlike many humans). It's simply the best time for a hunter to be in the woods.

Pre-rut is the stage leading up to full rut. This is when bucks start cruising a larger area, scoping out potential females and prime spots for opportunity.

Bucks start making rubs on trees and placing scrapes on the ground. (We'll cover more on that in a moment.) This activity is noticeably more prevalent than in the weeks and months prior. The bucks get very territorial, and thankfully, this gives hunters many useful clues to know that they are in the area. The bucks are usually eating heavily before the rut to be maximum size for the seasonal chaos. The bigger that they are, the better their competitive advantage in fighting, and also the longer they can chase and mate, lasting on their fat reserves. Their necks get noticeably larger, and their total weight reaches a peak size for the year.

READING THE SIGNS

Let's talk for just a few minutes about scrapes and rubs. A rub is a marking on the base of a small tree or group of trees. A buck uses his antlers to rub bark off of the tree, typically from about a foot off the ground to three feet high. When he rubs the tree, he is accomplishing multiple tasks. He is making a physical marking to let other deer know that he is claiming the spot as his own, or issuing a challenge to the resident buck or bucks in the area. He is marking the territory with his flag. Sometimes bucks will rub a tree totally bare at the base, and the virgin wood underneath becomes very visible, even from far away. The sight of the missing bark lets deer (and us) know that he is around. The other thing that is happening when he rubs a tree is that he is leaving his scent at the spot. The scent glands around his face leave traces of smell that other deer can pick up on and identify. He is also strengthening his neck muscles and maybe sharpening his tines in case a fight arises. Sometimes he will rub a bunch of trees in a cluster. He can snap a sapling in half. The rubs are usually placed in high traffic areas, or in a semi-open spot so that other deer will see it. Many people will argue this point, but it's almost impossible to know how big a buck is by looking at a rub. I have witnessed small bucks rub and rub and rub, decimating a tree. I have also seen big bruisers barely leave a mark. We cannot assume that all the rubs in an area are from the same buck either. What we do know is that only bucks do it. That helps. Many rubs concentrated in one area could mean that there are many bucks around, or maybe that there is just a single, very motivated one. Rubs do help us scout for bucks. They are another sign to monitor and take into account. The problem with a rub is that bucks don't typically return to the same one. This means hanging a stand beside a big rub may not necessarily increase our chances. Sometimes, however, a line of rubs can help identify a certain buck's preferred travel route.

Another buck sign that may be more useful in choosing a stand location is a scrape. A scrape is a marking on the ground. Bucks will clear a spot on the ground to expose raw earth underneath. This is almost always under a low-hanging limb in a well-traveled corridor. They want a totally clean scrape, with only dirt showing. It's typically about two feet wide but can be three times that size. This is a big help for us because leaves fall in the fall. That means the buck must clean up the scrape frequently to keep leaves and sticks out of it. So he will return to the spot for scrape maintenance and also monitor the doe activity around it. A scrape is not only a territory marker like a rub, but it also has another cool function. It's a method of communication between bucks and does. The buck makes his scrape, creating a bare spot in the dirt with his feet and sometimes his antlers. While scraping with his feet and raking away all the natural foliage on the ground, he simultaneously rubs his face, head, and antlers in the leaves and limbs just above it. He also chews on the attached leaves, without eating them or removing them. This leaves a lot of scent at the site. When a doe comes by, she checks out his handiwork and smells around. If she likes what she sees and smells, and is getting interested, she will urinate in the scrape. This is her way of letting the buck know that she is interested, and possibly getting close to a breeding opportunity. So the buck will check back to freshen up the scrape so that it presents well, and also to see if any does have left him a flirty message. If he picks up on her scent and can tell that she is almost ready, he will hang around the area more, checking back often, and try to locate her by smell. This means that you can hunt a scrape and have some expectation of him returning to the same spot.

The important thing to know about scrapes is that they are not a guarantee. A scrape is yet another advantageous tool to be used alongside the other hints and strategies. A scrape can be helpful, but it will rarely produce a mature buck sighting. Big bucks will often check at night and stay out of human sight. Another point that some people don't know is that any given scrape can be used by a number of different bucks. It's not exclusive to the deer that created it. Many deer will share it. I have camera evidence of eight or more different bucks using the same scrape in the same week. A scrape is a definitive sign that a buck is in the area, but like a rub, it doesn't tell you how big he is. Sometimes you can see the scrape and tell how many tines are on one side of his rack and how far apart the tips are. Sometimes you can see his entire footprint in the scrape, and other times, you may be able to tell how wide his toes are split apart by looking at the scrape marks in the dirt that he made with his foot. These clues help. Pay attention. Scrapes can be a perfect spot for surveillance with a trail camera, especially if it seems to be regularly used. However, we must resist the urge to check the scrapes too frequently. Every trip into the area is another chance for us to be seen, heard, or smelled. Remember, we want the bucks to do what they naturally want to do, not make changes based on something we did by mistake.

What about mock scrapes and rubs? Some hunters will manufacture a rub themselves using a pair of shed antlers or an old rack from a previous kill. Other people will make mock scrapes using a rake, a deer leg, antlers, or sticks. Some people also hang a scent dripper over the scrape. Here is my take on that stuff. By now, you can probably anticipate what I am about to say. I think hunters like to tinker too much. I think making a fake rub or scrape is more likely to hurt you than to help you. It is likely that the area will smell like a human afterward, not a rutting buck. Returning back regularly to freshen the scrapes up is likely a bad idea. Does the scent in the scent dripper smell authentic, like a real Georgia doe in heat? I have no idea. Is there a chance deer will smell our human scent too? Absolutely! Trying to trick a buck into thinking that another buck is on his turf isn't as easy as some people think. Rutting bucks have a serious, strong odor and lay that scent down everywhere they travel. If that scent is missing, mature bucks will likely notice that something is fishy. I'm certain that human breath doesn't smell like deer breath, so don't try chewing those limbs over the scrape either.

When rut is in full swing, you will likely see evidence of it. The bucks and the does begin to emit different, strong hormonal chemicals from their scent glands that even a human can smell when close by. Bucks will be chasing does all over the place. The does make them work for it a little bit and lead them around in hot pursuit. When multiple deer are running around in the woods, they are much easier to see and hear. Sometimes it's flat-out crazy out there. The action is intense and very frequent. If you are lucky enough to be in an area of the property where a hot doe is hanging out, you are in for a treat. This is the one time of the year that bucks are careless. They have one thing on their minds and immediately forget every-thing that their mothers taught them, just like teenage boys on Spring Break in Panama City Beach. They will run into an area without caution. During rut, you will see bucks that you haven't seen all year. They may be bucks that have been keeping a low profile on your farm, or may be one that crusaded from another farm, miles away. Checking the cameras around rut time is always exciting because new targets show up that you don't recognize. It's an amazing time.

The last thing that I want to say about rut is that when the rut action is on, you have to be there! Many hunters will overhunt in early season when chances are slim, and conditions aren't very favorable. They may burn out themselves, burn out their spots, or burn out their spouses. So when rut finally arrives, they aren't taking advantage of the opportunity. This is absolutely the best time to see a big buck, if not several of them. Make the most of this time. Be there and be smart about it. It's also a time to sit during different times of the day. Many big bucks are killed during the middle of the day during rut. Don't be afraid to stay out there all day if you have a hot spot and perfect conditions.

PERFECT TIMING

Many hunters get confused on when the rut occurs. If you listen to the old guy at the diner, he'll tell you one thing, and your brother-in-law will tell you something else. The best thing to do is to trust actual science, not local opinion. Does come into heat at different parts of the fall season in different parts of the country; timing can vary by weeks or months. Furthermore, even within the state of Georgia it can vary county by county, and be weeks or months apart between two areas of the state. There is not a general "Georgia" rut time, but there is a specific time for each specific area. The southern half of your county could be ten days behind the northern portion. Wildlife biologists in our state keep tabs on these dates and changes. They use the age of fawns born in different parts of the state to backtrack and determine when the deer were conceived and born. This provides accurate ovulation times, and tell us when the does were in heat last year, and provides an accurate prediction of when they should be in heat the year following.

Search the internet and find current, updated rut charts and maps. If you hunt in multiple counties or have access to different parts of the state, you can hunt numerous different rut periods and have the season of your life. Find a buddy in another part of the state and visit him during his rut and hunt, then invite him down to hunt your rut during your peak time. I do this almost every year. I am able to hunt Harris County, Schley County, Calhoun County, then Early County and have almost a month of full rut without having to drive more than 90 miles.

Many people in my hometown of Arlington will tell you that rut is always the week after Thanksgiving, but they are two weeks off, and I have confirmed their error year after year. They hunt hard during the wrong week and then claim that the bucks just aren't running any does this year. They assume that their deer numbers are falling apart because of the lack of intense activity. Two weeks later, when they are sitting home watching football, bucks are going bananas, and I'm in the woods enjoying every minute of the beautiful chaos. A great scouting tactic is to develop a relationship with a few local deer processing owners or employees. They can give you reports and let you know when the big bucks start rolling in. One of my processors told me that he went from processing three mature bucks a week for three weeks and then received 40 mature deer the very next week. It's like flipping a switch. When it's on, it's on, and you need to be out there. I call or stop in to talk to the processor weekly to get reports, even outside of the rut. They will tell me the recent harvest numbers, and whether morning or afternoons have been better, and I can correlate data and tighten up my game plan. In general, I hunt less than most of my peers but enjoy equal or better success because I get out there when there are higher probabilities for big results.

Study the state research rut data and know your areas and dates. Stop listening to non-credible sources. See what's in the local cooler and keep tabs on the area. Combining these factors will probably make for the best hunting week of your life.

This heavy beast was taken during the first few days of peak rut. The does trickled into the food plot first, and about fifteen minutes later, this bruiser ran into view to check the does to see if any of them were ready for his services. He stayed in the field for about two minutes, running from one doe to the next. He only stopped moving once, just before he was headed back into cover. That's all I needed.

CHAPTER 11
Scouting the Territory

W hen scouting a potential hunting territory, there are many things to look for. We hope to find evidence of many deer using the property, especially mature bucks. Obviously, tracks, trails, excrement, antler sheds, rubs, scrapes, consumed foliage, and deer sightings help indicate how much activity is there. Walking a property can tell you a great deal about the activity there. It's harder to read the land in the summertime months because there is less deer activity, and the plants regrow and recover so quickly. In the fall and winter, you can tell much more about the place. The advantageous thing about scouting in the spring and summer is that you don't have to worry as much about messing up a hunting spot. The spring is the best time to find antler sheds. Before everything starts to become green again, you can cover a ton of ground and also see a long way in the deer woods. Usually, the antlers have dried out some and are easy to spot because of the whiter color. If you perform prescribed burns on the property, looking for sheds just after the burn makes it easier to find sheds. A wide open charred space is easy to cover quickly, and the antlers can often show up from far away. Finding sheds is a great way to know which bucks likely made it through the season. It also gives a definitive sign that he was using that particular area. This is useful info for the upcoming season. If you are also a hunter of the Eastern Turkey in our state, be sure to keep a lookout for sheds when chasing toms. This is a great time to pick a few up.

In the later spring and summer months, it's still a smart idea to get out and see what's happening. Just stay cool and watch out for snakes. The scouting data can be very useful in the early months to take inventory of the deer herd and to see where they are hanging out. However, the deer patterns will likely change a great deal once the thermometer starts dropping towards the end of the year. In the warm months, you are mostly looking for worn down trails, tracks, and deer feces because the deer are not making rubs and scrapes during that time. Tracks can give you an idea of how many bucks and does are around, and show how big they may be. These warm months are the time when the bucks are in velvet, growing their racks, and the fawns are being raised by their mothers. It's a great time get some neat pictures. We'll talk about cameras in a bit.

In the fall, we can start gathering some more valuable intel. If possible, I recommend using your scent eliminator while scouting all year, but be certain to use it as deer season gets within a month away. Spray everything down with scent eliminator. Enter and exit the woods just like when you are hunting. As the bucks start shedding their velvet, they will start making some rubs, but not as many as in the rut and pre-rut stage. They will start moving more, eating more, and developing patterns. It's smart to sit on food sources and watch from a distance before the season comes in. During the late summer and early fall, bucks will often travel in groups by age class. Similar bucks will hang out together. That means that if you get a chance to see a giant, you may get to see a few of his mature buddies too. Laying eyes on your targets is good for confirmation, recognition, and pure adrenaline. The first time you see a prime target buck for the year, whether on camera or in person, it's a rush. Then the personal challenge really begins.

As I said before, rubs are a sign that bucks are using the area, but not an indicator of how big they are. Tracks are an accurate indicator of age and body size, but not necessarily the rack size. The same group of six does can use an area all week, and it can look like 1,000 deer have been there, not knowing how long the hoof prints have been there. Scouting within 48 hours of a heavy rain is always helpful because you get a clean slate and can decipher when the tracks were left. Scouting with 12 hours or less of rain can also tell you which direction the deer travel at different times the day. For instance, if it stopped raining at 5:30 a.m. and you see a bunch of tracks, all pointing west, at 8:45 a.m., you know that those deer traveled in a westward direction in the morning. On the TV shows, you will see where the hunters identify a bedding area and a food source and the deer just bounce back and forth on schedule. In most areas of Georgia, this is not the case because there are many bedding areas and a large supply of food. It's not that simple. However, even if you do not know exactly where they are heading or where they departed from, a lot of deer will travel in a general direction in the morning, and in the opposite direction in the afternoon. If your farm shows these type of patterns, you can certainly use the info to your advantage. Many farms in Georgia exhibit these general patterns.

I harvested this buck in a tight spot where only a long rifle shot was possible. This buck left numerous tracks crossing the same spot on a firebreak for weeks. The camera confirmed that on the mornings that he came through, he had been traveling westward, after 9:00 a.m., and was usually the last of many deer to come through. I couldn't get close to this spot without an extremely noisy trek. I sat in a stand that allowed me quiet access but required a long shot. It all worked out one cold morning at about 9:15 a.m.

Using Trail Cameras

Modern trail cameras may have been the best and the worst thing that has happened to whitetail hunting. The pros outweigh the cons for sure, and the cons can certainly be controlled. The reason why cameras are the best thing is obvious. They allow surveillance of the landscape and provide us with invaluable information, even when we don't have time to be on the property. More still, we can survey the property without physical presence and time in the tree. We can learn the buck to doe ratios, how many animals are using the area, what time they arrive and leave, and what they all look like. Camera photos help us decide which bucks we want to harvest and which ones need more time. Having multiple pictures helps tremendously. It helps us to eliminate mistakes and avoid shooting the wrong deer. After all, they usually look way bigger in real life. We get trigger happy and then find out the hard way that "ground shrinkage" is a real thing. Shooting a deer that is too young is a regrettable mistake.

The bad thing about trail cameras is that once we positively identify a stud shooter on the memory card, we innately want to storm in there and get him. This often turns into emotional, overzealous decision-making, and we trek into the spot at the wrong time, when conditions aren't favorable, or we frequent it too often, and force the deer to move from the area. Overhunting a trophy deer is a costly mistake. It takes discipline to hold out and wait for the right opportunity.

If you plan to use a trail camera, and I hope you do, there needs to be a few camera strategies. Putting multiple cameras out is awesome if you can afford to do so. Keep a log of all the bucks, where they showed up, and what time they showed up. This data sometimes looks random, but in time can reveal valuable patterns. Study the pictures and get to know the bucks, so that when they show up, you know which one it is and do not have to make a rushed judgment call. Have your hit-list established and studied as much as possible. Trust me, dutiful preparation in learning your deer inventory is massively important. These images and videos should be studied to identify not only which deer are the shooters and non-shooters, but also what unique features about each deer will help you to identify them faster. Sometimes, all you have a chance to see is one fleeting glimpse of a deer when hunting. You may only get to view one side of his rack, or possibly only one tine. If you already know the buck from studying his pictures, you can quickly look for distinguishing characteristics, like a split brow tine on one side or an inwardly-curved G3 tine, and decisively charge ahead and take the shot. If you don't already know that deer, and you need another look or two to decide whether to shoot, you may not get the chance.

As far as cameras are concerned, there are many options and price ranges. They are being improved and updated every year. The original trail camera introduced many years ago was $450 and took 24 pictures on film that had to be removed and developed. Now you can spend less than $100 and get a camera that will take 10,000 pictures with no flash. You can decide on what to buy based on features and prices. I don't have a favorite. My recommendation is to get one with a strong warranty and favorable reviews online. The thing that absolutely does matter is whether or not the camera has a motion sensing light or some light that stays on for more than a millisecond. Some cameras have one small, dim light that is meant to illuminate the field of view for the no-flash capture. Others have a small, dim, motion detecting light that comes on when game is in front of it. For whatever reason, these lights that are visible, and come on and off in front of the deer, really bother them. I have seen it time and time again. They will stare at it. If every picture of your deer is one of them staring at the camera, it's probably because they are a little curious, bothered, or scared of it.

Whatever type of camera you use, and however many you use, keep in mind that long battery life and larger storage capacity means fewer trips into the woods. This is vitally important. If you sweep in to check a camera once or twice every week, you are making a mistake. Your repeat visits lessen your chances of killing a big buck. I also recommend a camera with a multi-shot feature, like the ones that take three quick pictures instead of just a single shot. When you slink in to retrieve cameras or memory cards, spray down and treat it just like a hunt. But please hear me on this. Control yourself. I know it's exciting to get new pictures, but we must show discipline and self-control. Be patient. Buy cameras with extended battery life and let them stay there for long periods of time. Leave them for a month at a time. Start in the summertime and begin to take inventory early. Watching them grow is exciting. Don't force any deer to change patterns. Remember, we want them to act natural, and eventually, we will be there waiting when the time is right. You don't want to push them off of the property because they get wise or worried.

This old deer, which we named "Splits," is a prime example of a buck with unique features that were identified using trail cameras. His split G2 on the right side and multiple brown tines made him recognizable in an instant. After multiple pictures were captured, he was added to the hit list. I encountered him from the stand very briefly during pre-rut without a shot opportunity, and he was harvested two weeks later during peak rut.

CHAPTER 12
Supplemental Nutrition

W hat's the best way to feed the herd and keep the deer happy?

We will discuss how to feed deer, but I want to make one point before we get there. If you have extra cash to spend on protein, minerals, corn, beans, etc., that is just fine. Supplementing feed can only help the herd. However, the most important component to whether or not you grow big bucks is genetics, not nutrition. A deer with inferior genetics cannot be fed more protein and become a true giant. You can burn a lot of money on feeding deer, but focusing on improving genetics is the most important factor. Feeding can make a small difference, but don't expect miracles to come from the high-priced protein blend.

There are many ways to try to provide nourishment for a deer herd and give them reasons to stick around.

In our state, it's now legal to feed deer by many means, and in certain zones, we are even permitted to hunt directly over it. When the baiting law first passed, people were in uproar, thinking that it would decimate the deer population and make it too easy to kill big bucks. People argued against it, claiming that it would take the sport out of hunting. So what happened to the harvest numbers when people began dumping corn, minerals, treats, and protein feed by the ton? Nothing. Much to the surprise of many hunters and politicians, the harvest numbers didn't significantly change. That's because deer adapt. They will certainly partake in your free and easy food source, but it won't be their only food source, and they will consume it with their naturally timid and paranoid survival skills still intact. They know if you've been around and will certainly adjust to your presence. There is no guaranteed, easy street for killing giant bucks. They are just too smart. They may decide to exclusively eat in the dark when they know the food is available.

I have a few tips for planting and feeding. Let's start with good old-fashioned food plot planting. Luckily for us in this great state, commercial agriculture is abundant across the land. This provides extra food during many months of the year. If you hunt on or near an active farm, this can only help your herd. In the south, peanuts can be a magnet for deer in several growing and harvesting phases. Corn or soybeans can be a major asset and a preferred food source too. Our deer also feed on millet, wheat, oats, rye, sorghum, and even cotton plants. If these crops are near you, scout around the fields and find access points with lots of tracks. Put up cameras to see what is using the field and when they are using it. Plot watching, time-lapse type cameras can be a real advantage on bigger fields. These allow a picture to be taken every few minutes of the entire field and don't rely exclusively on close proximity motion to trigger the camera shutter. We must continuously monitor agricultural fields because they can transform from zero activity to party central overnight. I recommend sitting on large fields from a safe distance before season comes in, and during season with binoculars or a spotting scope to scout the place to determine where deer enter the field and when. You can sit under an irrigation pivot or even on a tractor if you don't have stands up yet. In early season, you can often sit at a distance in your truck without bothering the animals. Once you get some wildlife patterns figured out, you can fine-tune a stand setup to capitalize on your research findings.

I am a fan of feeding by the bagful, but food plots have to be the next best thing for whitetails behind big, commercial agricultural production. If you have the time, equipment, and finances, plant as many food plots as you can and make them as big as you possibly can. A common mistake that hunters make is making them too small. Generally, smaller plots make deer feel less safe. Deer take comfort in having other deer around. A big plot full of deer is a magical place for opportunity to find you. The other obvious factor with small plots is that they can't support the nutritional needs of as many animals. More food means more deer can survive in any given area. They want the easiest food source. Feasting over tasty greens, beets, beans, corn, and radishes and filling their tank in a few minutes is much better than grazing briars for a few hours. It's hard to grow flourishing food plots in Georgia because of the extreme heat, variable rainfall, and prevalent weeds. The soil may be unproductive, and sometimes we just sustain too long without water. It's a risk. Plant what you can afford to lose and know that some or all of it will be lost some years. I recommend planting a mixture of things in the same plot. If you have a 60-yard wide strip that's 100 yards long, plant three different crops down the plot, each 20 yards wide. This diversifies the plot, maximizes your chances of something turning out well, and gives the deer multiple options. In time, you will learn what items grow best in what areas, and also learn what the deer prefer. In the early season, try iron clay peas (cowpeas), soybeans, corn, sorghum, clover, and oats. (Stay away from alfalfa in the southern half of the state.) Try to plant right before rain is forecast to show up and use a broad spectrum or recommended fertilizer. Corn and sorghum will need higher nitrogen levels to produce well. Sorghum is easier to grow than corn, but probably not as preferred by the deer. You can do a soil test or use a pH monitor to see if other soil amendments or minerals are needed. In the pre-winter months, you can sow or drill in your rye, oats, wheat, radishes, turnips, collards, rape, and more. There are many convenient plot mixes on the market today, just know that everything on the bag won't grow well on your lease.

Native forage for the deer is often low in vitamins and minerals, especially during summer drought or in cold, late winter. The most critical time to feed and supplement your deer is after a stress period when native forage is inferior to your plots or other feeds. High-quality spring nutrition is important because this is when fawns are being born and nursed, causing a higher need for nutrition for the mother and the babies. It's also when antlers start growing on your bucks. Better nutrition can certainly help antler growth. However, premium nutrition is impactful to antler growth from the time they drop their antlers in late winter, all the way to the time when they drop the velvet on their next rack after the summer. In winter, right after the rut comes blasting through, the bucks are malnourished and exhausted, and the does are now becoming pregnant. This is a time when we need to have adequate nutrition available for the herd, and many hunters neglect it as the hunting season ends.

If you use mineral blocks or supplemented feed, be sure to make them available to deer during the times when they need it most, not just during hunting season. You will likely see that your mineral sites will get visited more frequently during these critical times, and may even be abandoned during other periods of the year. A healthy herd produces better deer. If a malnourished buck gets sick or is lacking critical nutrients, it will affect his antler growth. We want him and all the other deer to be healthy all year long. The mother deer need heightened nutrition from mid-fall to late summer to develop, birth, and feed healthy fawns. Bucks need superior food sources to prepare for rut in the mid-fall, and to recover in late winter.

Males also need a superior diet from early spring to early fall to achieve optimal antler growth.

So what about pouring the feed bag, loading big feeders, or riding across the lease with the side-dump feed trailer gate wide open? I say "Yes! Feed away!" to all of them. Do it as much as you can afford to do it, as long as you can maintain it. Just know that it can get expensive, and it will not necessarily guarantee more kills. A high-protein and high-fat diet produce better deer, but where we live, your feeding may not produce measurable results because the deer will eat from many sources, not just exclusively from your feed trough. Just think of it as a supplement. The key is that the higher level of supplemental feed needs to be maintained to keep healthy numbers on the land. Over time, you will see small improvements from your efforts. Most land managers would agree that more food is exponentially better than less for seeing more deer. Where I differ from many hunters and managers is the method for how to feed. If you are intending to feed, I have a few recommendations that seem to produce favorable hunting results.

If you plan to feed using standing feeders, you have a few options. You can use a trough, a tripod style hopper feeder, a hanging feeder, or some sort of pipe feeder. If you have unwanted hogs and you are exclusively trying to grow deer, this can get real expensive. The pigs eat like crazy. If the feed hits the ground or is in a reachable trough or pipe, they will consume everything and run the deer away to do so. So if you have hogs, you should use an on-demand feeder that is out of reach of the hogs. You will likely need to stake the legs down or keep it heavily filled so they can't knock it over. They will try. If you don't have hogs, you have many more options for feeding deer. People assume that hopper style feeders that spin and throw feed at certain times of the day will train deer to feed at those times. However, trail camera research shows that if the feed is on the ground, deer will just leave it there and come to it at the time that they would normally feed, which is typically after hours. There is nothing wrong with this type of feeder, just don't expect the timer to change the deer's normal feeding pattern too much. It may also just be a dinner bell for other rodents and opportunistic animals.

Many modern land managers prefer an on-demand style, gravity-fed, raised feeder. It saves money on wet feed getting stuck in the mud and rotting and prevents feeding overstuffed raccoons and squirrels. It also allows the deer do what they want to do without adding extra noise from a motor. Let them come and go on their schedule and get comfortable. Sometimes they will come at night and sometimes during the day. Either way, don't expect it to perform miracles and get mature buck to show up to the buffet with no survival instincts. Often, a feeding site will cause deer to be more cautious and worried. I'm not saying that you can't hunt over them, just that you will probably be more effective if you stay away from them and allow the deer to get comfortable in the area. If your camera shows consistent daylight patterns of a target deer, then make a hunting plan near that location. There is also an advantage with these on-demand devices because you don't have to worry about wiring connections, batteries, or solar panels. The key to these feeders is volume. Get the big one and fill it up, ensuring that you don't have to make trip after trip back to the spot to refill. Remember, less human presence is always the goal. Furthermore, if you are planning to feed, don't just do it for a few weeks here and a few weeks there. Maintain a constant food supply for months on either side of the season and keep them full all year if possible. Never give up an opportunity to leave a trail camera at the feeder sites. Constant surveys are valuable, even if you aren't planning to hunt this exact spot. It's important to keep an accurate inventory of the deer on the property.

Often, we want to feed in an area that we don't want to put a feeder or can't plant a food plot. No problem. I understand completely. In these cases, you can walk a few bags or buckets of feed back to your secret spot and pour it out. The key here again is volume. In a busy spot with high traffic, deer can eat a five-gallon bucket of corn in just a day, especially if it's in one pile. If you are going this route, put enough in the area to last a while, so you don't need to return over and over to replenish the stash. The risk of putting a large amount out is rain, mold, and rot. Something that I find works well is to scatter the corn all over the area, being careful not to put it in lower, wet spots. Instead of eating a pound of corn in one pile without lifting their head, let the deer graze around just like they naturally do for acorns and other natural forage. Scatter it all over the place. I wish I had a long-range corn sprayer for these applications. Maybe drone delivery will be possible in the future.

Remember to treat your boots, clothes, and gloves with the scent protecting techniques that we already talked about, and then make it rain corn. The feed will last much longer this way before it's all gobbled up. I will go one step further to admit that I like to keep it moving every few weeks. When I return to freshen up the treats, I always move it to another area, still in strategic position for where I plan to hunt, but not in the exact spot as last time. Move it a hundred yards or so. This gets the deer into a grazing pattern instead of a dash in and dash out, nocturnal, fast-food, practice. My trail camera research also shows that a pile of corn is more likely to get hit at night, but scattered corn is likely to be browsed with some daylight still left. That's a big win for the hunter.

CHAPTER 13
Taking Aim

We've talked a great deal about how to prepare, where to setup, and what to do to see more deer. Now we need to discuss which ones to shoot when they finally show up. You will find numerous strategies and modalities from different hunters on this issue. I hope to debunk some of the common misconceptions, point out some common mistakes, and provide you with a sure-fire system that you can confidently implement.

Misconception #1 - Shoot spikes, they will never amount to anything. This is total bull. Most deer with just two points, typically called spikes, are very young. You can look at their body and tell that they are young (more on this in a few paragraphs). The spikes are normally the first "rack" they have ever grown. Sure, I would like to see a first-year deer have 8-10 points, but most of them don't. With adequate time, spikes can certainly turn into gigantic, trophy bucks. I'm not saying that everyone does, but they certainly could. A young spike is in no way a predictor of future growth. There is no way to know at this stage if he has inferior genetics. He needs more time. The only time we should consider shooting a spike is if he is badly injured, or if he is obviously very old. The latter case is extremely rare. If a five-year-old deer is a spike, you probably don't want him breeding in your herd. However, in all my year's hunting, I may have seen a legitimately old spike twice. If he's 220 pounds with a pot belly and stands over the other six deer in the field, take him. Otherwise, stay away from spikes and let them grow.

Misconception #2 - When meat hunting, shoot the biggest doe. I understand that you want the biggest bang for your buck, or in this case, the biggest doe for the bang. If you are laboring to drag, skin, gut, and process a deer, you want to make it worth the time and the money. Hear me out on this one. Most people just look at buck genetics when trying to grow their herd, and fail to think about the other 50% contributor to the genetic equation. The doe accounts for a great deal on whether to not a future record-breaker is conceived. If Shaquille O'Neil and Venus Williams were to have a baby, there is a high probability that their offspring will be large. If Shaq and a typical, much smaller, woman were to have a child, there is a higher chance that the offspring would be smaller than the one born to Venus Williams. If a small man and a small woman have a child, they are most likely to have a much smaller baby than either of the previous two examples. The bottom line is this: Don't shoot your biggest, tallest, most robust does if you are serious about improving your deer herd quality and raising bigger bucks.

Talk to a purebred cattleman or a deer breeder about how to produce the best animals, and you will learn about the importance of selecting superior females to achieve greatness. It's never just about having a great bull or a stud buck. Most deer breeders will spend more money on their doe herd than they do the bucks. Buck size is largely dependent on the mother doe. There are some intangibles in the DNA equation for a hunter that isn't raising deer in a pen and keeping detailed breeding records, but top-notch breeders know that certain does produce wide-racked deer and certain does produce taller-racked deer. We can't control everything, but we need to consider all the variables.

If there are many does in the field, and you want to shoot a doe, select one that is in the middle of the pack, not the most genetically superior one. Keep the Venus Williams doe in the club as long as possible. You want those mega does to have as many offspring as possible. If you hone your skills of aging deer, then try to also shoot the older does over the younger ones.

Misconception #3 - Don't shoot him if he doesn't have at least 4 points on one side. This is a practice that many hunting clubs live by, and some municipalities, counties, and states legally require. The ongoing research shows that over time, this rule can hurt your deer herd and reduce the genetic quality of the bucks. Hear me out. It makes total sense once you take a moment to think it through. If all the hunters are having to pass on buck after buck, anxiously waiting for one that has more than 4 points on one side, when one finally shows up, he probably gets blasted. This may be a two-year-old 11-point that scores 110", with the potential to be a 160" class deer in 3 years. He's now gone, removing the chance for him to reach his full potential, but even worse, preventing him from impregnating multiple does every year and passing on his superior genetic qualities. You don't just lose one great buck; you potentially could be losing a dozen of them over the next few years. So these restrictions can force club members to shoot genetically superior deer too early. We never want that.

The second major component that makes the four on one side practice a dangerous policy is if the deer genetically predisposed to be 5, 6, and 7 points never get removed, eventually, you have an entire herd of big 6-points. That's all that survives to pass on the bad traits. We are killing the best genetics and only keeping the bad ones. I would encourage you to shoot every mature (by age) 5, 6, 7, and 8-points that you see, regardless of the rack size. The way to grow a herd is to commit to passing on the 10,11,12, and 13-pointers until they reach 4 or 5 years of age so that you have better genetics multiplying in your herd. If you commit to this, it takes a few years to see results, but those results will blow your mind. I've seen it time and again. Landowners will say that they can't grow anything but 7 and 8-pointers, then on year four, observing the right management program, they start seeing 10's left and right. If you live in a regulated zone, you must follow the law. If you have the option to shoot what you want, remove the mature bucks with bad racks, and allow the ones with promising potential to stay. It's hard to pass up a beautiful 130 inch, three-year-old, 11-point. I have had to do it many times. It's also hard to "waste" a tag on a 180 pound, five-year-old, 6-point. It will be worth it in time. I promise. Try to get everyone that hunts with you and around you to get on the same management program. Form a co-op with other farms if you can. Everyone wins if there is a big block of joined property observing smart harvest practices.

This old, wide 6-point had been on the property for years and was almost exclusively nocturnal. I never had a picture of him in daylight hours. He was a prime example of a hit list buck that needed to be removed for management purposes. I finally seized a chance to take him very late one evening with just enough shooting light to positively identify him. By then, he had lost a brow tine to fighting, which made him the biggest 5-point I had ever witnessed.

Misconception #4 - Don't shoot him unless he is "outside the ears." This rule, as well as rule #3, is often used to prevent someone from shooting a deer that's too small. These may be some decent guidelines for a novice hunter to protect young deer. I get it. The problem is that a lot of young deer are wide enough to meet the criteria before they reach their full potential. That means that they may get shot too early. The flip side can also be true, that you have a mature, aged, deer that needs to be removed, but he isn't wide enough. Depending on what position the buck is currently holding his ears, it can also be difficult to tell how wide he is. What if you never get an angle to judge his spread? That happens often. You'll discover as you encounter more big bucks that you often have a very fleeting moment of a single angle to make the call. Either way, just like the previous example, this rule can result in some deer being killed too early and allow others to get a free pass when they should be shot. It can also result in favorable genetics disappearing and unfavorable ones taking over. The solution is to shoot the correct, old, mature deer, regardless of the number of tines and the number of inches between them.

Misconception #5 - Shoot all the ugly ones. They are "cull" bucks.

Many hunters look for an excuse to shoot a deer because they are trigger happy. They will roll up to the local deer processing facility, claiming that the buck on the tailgate was a cull buck. Hear me out on this point. Just because a deer looks weird this year, doesn't mean that he will be that way next year. Many deer have a nutritional deficiency during a key point in antler growth. Some of them get injured before their antlers are fully developed. Some of them get sick, and it manifests in poor rack formation. In all of these cases, the problem is likely temporary and will be different next year if conditions improve. If he is old enough and you can confirm that there is a genetic problem, and it's not just a fluke, then fire away.

How do we know for sure if it's a cull or just a bad year? The best way to know is to monitor cameras and pay attention to what you observe each year. If you have a deer that has had the same deficiencies on the same side of his rack year after year, then it's likely a genetic problem. If you have multiple deer, at multiple stages of development that all exhibit the same bad trait, it's probably genetic. I hunted a farm years ago where I had about six bucks from age two to six that all had an 8-point main beam frame on the right side and three spikes on the left with no beam shape. They were obviously related. I tried to harvest as many of these animals as possible and was confident that it was a sensible management plan.

Annual harvest timing matters too. If you do identify some older cull bucks, it's best to try to harvest them earlier in the year. If you have confirmation of some undesirable genetics, you want to remove that deer before the rut when he will be breeding many times. The first week of gun season may be the best time to get the job done. If you get a chance to take him later, that's fine, but try to do it as quickly as possible once you decide that he is on the hit list.

We have debunked a few common mistakes and

bad ideas, now let's talk about the right way to shoot. Before we start aligning the crosshairs, we have to do some homework. We must spend time looking at photos, reading, watching videos, and talking with other hunters and game processors to effectively learn how to judge a deer's age. Age is the foremost criteria on whether or not we should shoot a buck. We cannot make an assessment of his genetic quality until we know he is at his peak age and has had a chance to exhibit his full potential. In a breeding facility with controlled genetics, a deer can be judged sooner. In the wild, we have no idea who his parents were, so we have to give him a chance to grow. There are many articles, videos, and other materials that will help you learn to age deer on the hoof. The overall body shape of a buck can be the most indicative component to assessing age. When you have the right things to look for on body shape and size, then you can begin to add in other factors. A deer's overall girth, his belly size, shoulder structure, hips, length, and even his facial structure are all indicators of his age. Once these items are noticed, the circumferences of his antler bases, the length of his beams, the mass of his tines, and number of extra points, kickers, and stickers can help solidify the judgment. There are a lot of factors to study, and it can be very difficult to assess a deer walking by in the brush when you have only 4 seconds, and your heart is racing. That's why having trail camera pictures and studying them is invaluable. If you know that your target buck has a remarkable, double, left brow tine or a squiggly G3, you can pick him out faster and make a quick decision. In contrast, if you have a few deer that look great at first glance, but aren't quite old enough, it's advantageous to be able to recognize them too, so that a spur of the moment, wrong decision isn't made. Having many pictures from different angles is invaluable to study and evaluate your deer.

My recommendation is to never shoot a buck under 3.5 years old. Yes, I said never. If he is 3.5, has thick bases but only 4 points, has poor tine length, is missing brow tines, or exhibits some other traits that lead you to believe that he won't ever be a stud, then you can take him. However, if he's awesome at 3.5, the goal is to give him two more years. It will be hard to pass him up at 4.5, and you may want to take him then if he's the best buck that you have ever had an opportunity to take. I appreciate that too. Just know that I have seen first-hand that a 130-140 inch, four-year-old can add 15-25 inches in a single year and be a show-stopper if given a pass.

In summary, we must allow bucks to reach an age where we can more accurately determine their potential. It's too hard to tell in the first few years, so we have to give them time to develop before we decide. Once he reaches an appropriate age for judging, we either shoot because he needs to be removed to improve the genetics of the herd, or we shoot because he is a trophy at his full potential. That's it. Remember that deer almost always look bigger from the tree. If you are on the fence, trying to figure out if he's big enough, he probably isn't. The first look should be a "Holy Moly! There he is!" moment.

This incredible 8-point known as "Sky High" was on my hit list all season. I could not believe how tall he was. When I finally got a chance to see him from the stand, there was no mistaking that it was him. I saw his rack coming through the brush minutes before I saw his body. It was an adrenaline-pumping moment for sure. So much so that I missed him. Uggh! My stomach hurts just thinking about it. I lost the lease after that year. He was killed by a guest on the property the next year, only after he had grown four more measurable points.

DOE MANAGEMENT

How do we know when to shoot does and how many should we shoot? You will undoubtedly get varying answers to these questions if you ask multiple hunters and land managers. I know some folks that never shoot does, claiming they want every doe to drop two fawns and for there to be deer everywhere. Some say that it's just a numbers game and that having more does increases the chance of birthing an awesome buck. Other managers subscribe to the idea that having less does forces bucks to travel more during rut, increasing our chances of seeing one. After all, if the buck has does around every corner, he doesn't ever have to venture out looking for them and may never show himself.

Cultivating the right plan comes down to a few key variables. One vitally important component is food. In that subcategory, we must ask a few questions. How many acres do you have? How much natural food do you have on the land? How much can you supplement to maintain adequate nutrition? It comes down to an issue of resources. If you have more food, and more wooded acres of habitat, you can support a larger herd. If food is scarce, having higher numbers means that all the animals get less of the supply, and can fail to thrive. Many farms have lots of deer, but never produce big deer for this very reason. This is similar to the common problem that we survey in fishing ponds across the state. Too many fish can eliminate your ability to grow any big ones because there isn't enough space or resources. If you watch 20 does every time you hunt, but never find big bucks, it may be time to remove some females.

Another important variable is the buck to doe ratio. Some managers say that a 4:1, buck to doe ratio is the goal. Other serious hunters will say that their goal is 1:1. I will say that either of these situations would probably make for a great place to hunt. Unfortunately, a lot of farms in Georgia have something closer to a 10:1 ratio, and it's rare to see big bucks at those tracts. It may be that they don't exist because of too much competition for food, but it's more likely that they are there and just remain out of sight. If they aren't traveling during rut to seek out sexual partners, we probably won't see them. A 1:1 ratio produces a lot of competition between bucks for the limited number of does. This would lead to more activity from bucks fighting and competing. It could also mean that a dominant buck will attempt to run off many of the smaller ones.

There is no way to get a perfectly accurate survey number for how many deer you have and what the ratio is. However, if we pay attention, we can get an accurate sample picture of what's going on. If you keep records of your deer activity, you will begin to understand your herd better. Keep a notebook or a computer spreadsheet of your findings. Every time you get home from a hunt, record the location, date, and what you saw. Have a column for the total number of deer spotted, as well as how many were does and how many were bucks. Every time you check a trail camera, record the same info. Get everyone who hunts and scouts on the same property to do the same. Over time, you will start to get a better idea of your numbers and whether or not they are improving. They will change from year to year. You may decide one year to remove 20 does for proper balance, and then realize two years later that you can't afford to kill any. Most people don't shoot enough does and shoot too many of the wrong bucks. In keeping accurate records, you will also learn patterns of which areas and which times of the year seem to be best for hunting success. The bottom line is that keeping track of these things will make you a better land manager and a better hunter. Keep studying, analyzing, reading, and learning.

If you see 8-10 does for every buck, it's probably time shoot some does. If you work and work and never encounter any deer at all, or you see a buck or two for every doe, I wouldn't shoot anything but stud bucks. Based on your findings, you will have to make an informed decision. I would shoot for the 4:1 doe to buck ratio as a goal and keep adjusting in either direction until you get there. You may decide in time that you want to alter that goal number. Just keep tracking, so you know what you have and then can make the best decision. If you hardly ever observe fawns and yearlings, it would be smart to start supplemental feeding and also start looking into hunting predators.

Here's one final thought on shooting bucks and does. Overzealous land management can sometimes take the fun out of a family farm for a few years. Sometimes we need to make a few exceptions, just not too many. Strict management can cause disagreements and turn off young hunters if they feel like they aren't allowed to shoot anything. I want a child to be able to shoot a deer that they will be proud of. Even if it doesn't meet your management standards, you may want to permit some of the young hunters to harvest a younger deer. My personal rule for young visiting hunters is that if it's your first ever deer, you can shoot whatever you want. Seize the opportunity that makes you happy. Once you get your first deer under your belt, the standards need to be raised. It starts as a gift, then turns to responsibility. I have taken around 20 people to kill their first deer. It's one of my favorite things in the world to do. No matter what the animal looks like, they are exhilarated in the hunting moment and even more so after the recovery. Maybe their first deer was a 1.5-year-old, 4-point. Next year, I may allow them to take a 3-year-old, 8-point that they will mount and be proud of. After that, it's mature deer only. Regular shooting and management rules apply. You can't regress backward and take another young 4-point, or a smaller 8-point. You make the call on your property. I just want to caution you, so the interested child doesn't get turned off or discouraged. Teach them land management and discipline as they understand more. This sport is probably one of the single best things a young person could be doing with their time. If you care about them becoming a serious hunter, just remember that it needs to be fun in the beginning.

LOCATING YOUR TARGET BUCK

I have mentioned a so-called "target buck" a few times so far in this book. This is the buck, hopefully, multiple bucks, which you have identified and approved as a shooter. They are the ones on your hit list. It's always beneficial to have some of them identified early in the season. Some may be carry-overs from last year, and some may be new to the list. It's likely that you haven't identified every buck on the property yet, and also likely that new bucks will enter the area later in the season. If you haven't found your shooter yet, I want to give you a process to hopefully locate one, and then to zero in on him and his patterns using a very effective scouting technique.

If you aren't using trail cameras, you are at a big disadvantage. I would spend more money on cameras than on better clothing, high-dollar scopes and rifles, or other hunting accessories. It would be a major disservice not to use modern technology and implement the use of trail cameras. Trail cameras have to be the second most valuable modern innovation for Georgia deer hunting, next to scent eliminating spray. I remember the old days before scouting cameras. It was tough. Back then, we relied on deer sign, keen instinct, and trial and error, not knowing if there was a mature buck in the area or not. The ability to confirm that a mature deer is using an area dramatically improves your chances and eliminates many hours of sitting in inferior areas.

If you have one camera, use it. If you have more than one, use all of them. I am going to assume that you have a few cameras. To first take a survey and locate a big buck, place the cameras out on the property, spaced far apart, in different areas where you know that deer like to be. Spray your rubber boots with scent elimi-nator. You may want to wear your snake proof boots. It's best to do this survey in the late summer to start getting a feel for what's out there. If you can do it all summer long, it's fun to watch the velvet antlers grow. By August, your cameras should be out and collecting data. At this point in the year, you can usually tell how big the deer will be, even if he's still putting on a few more antler inches. On the first camera deployment, there needs to be a preferred food source in front of the cameras. The easiest, cheapest, and most reliable product for the job is shelled corn. You can load it in a feeder, or just put it out on the ground. Put at least a full bag of corn (typically 40 pounds) in front of each camera. If you have the resources, pour one bag in a pile about 15 yards in front of the camera, then spread a second bag in a 30-50-yard area around the pile. You want an area that is open enough to get clear photos, which may require some foliage trimming. Double check your camera settings and make sure they are turned on.

Then leave those spots alone for two weeks to take pictures. After two weeks, spray down again, return to the spots, and pull the memory cards to check the photos. If you have extra blank cards, just pull the used one and put the new one in. Double check battery and camera settings and replenish the corn in the same way that you did the first time. Then, leave everything alone for another two weeks.

When you get back to your computer or card reader, sort through the memory cards and see what you have. The times that the deer are feeding may not be as critical now as they will be later in the year, but keep track of the activity. If there are no shooters on the camera yet, don't panic. That doesn't mean that you don't have any trophy bucks on the property. The bucks this time of the year probably won't be traveling too much. They may eat, drink, and bed without getting outside of a few hundred-yard radius this time of year. If there are no shooters, check again in two weeks to see if any show up. If after four weeks of continuous feed there are no shooters, then consider moving the camera to a new area.

The bucks this time of year tend to group by age. If you see one two-year-old deer, you may find three more with him. If you locate a stud, he may have a buddy or two close by. They will separate later in the year, but early on, it can be super exciting to see several bucks together. Bow hunters have a unique opportunity to be there during the early season when the bucks are traveling in groups. The downside is that it's really hot and the bugs may be intolerable.

If you find a shooter, and he's showing up daily, you are way ahead of the game, and you should start considering where to hang an early season stand. If a shooter shows up, but he is infrequent, it's time to reposition some cameras. From the location where you get a picture of an infrequent hit list buck, put out two or three more cameras and feed sites in different directions about 200-300 yards from that site. Remember, he isn't seeking to travel too much. The goal is to find his home location. Every waypoint where you can get a photo gives you more clues to his habits and whereabouts. If the original spot had two pictures, then we need to determine which direction he likes to hang out. By deploying three cameras in three directions fairly close by, we can dial our location efforts in a little more.

In this example, the center star is the original spot where two pictures were obtained. The numbered stars are the new positions added by deploying more cameras.

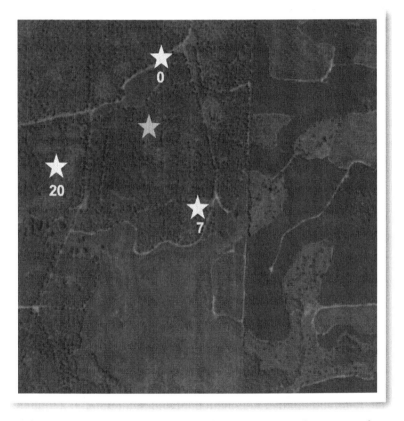

If the new spot to the north yielded zero pictures, the spot to the southwest grabbed 20, and the spot to the east captured 7, then you know that his general area is south of your original camera location. Now you can reposition again surrounding this area to start gathering information to attempt to find some patterns.

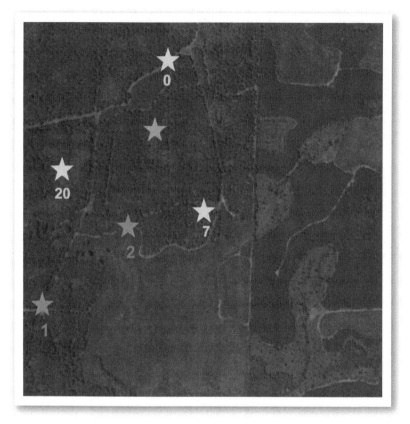

Stars 1 and 2 mark two potential locations to deploy cameras in an attempt to further target your buck's preferred home area.

Survey after survey may only give you random data, but sometimes it can reveal a repeatable pattern. He may show up on one camera exclusively in the mornings, and another only at night. This will give you some indication of how he moves in the area. If you have three or four cameras getting consistent pictures, then you can really start to put together a routine. Just keep moving the cameras until you confidently figure out where he is living.

This same camera technique can be used later in the season, but I like to do it early because if he is in a steady routine and showing up during hunting hours, you have a heightened chance to kill him in the first few weeks of the season. If you don't kill him during the first few weeks, your next best chance could be months away. If you can keep them running, let the cameras work all season. Keep tabs on your shooters and continue to try to find other ones on the property.

CHAPTER 14
These Boots Were Made for Walking

We talked about ground hunting before. In that section, I was talking about finding a spot and sitting on the ground for the full duration of the hunt. I want to take a few minutes to talk about a powerful tactic that most Georgia hunters never use. The spot and stalk method of hunting big game is mostly used out west on mountain tops and open plains, but I can tell you with confidence that if you practice and become proficient at it, it's a weapon that produces results here too. Perhaps a more common term for this style of hunting in the Southeast is "still hunting." I have killed many deer using still hunting methods. I want to share some of the basics with you. This should only be used if you know every inch of the farm. It's imperative to know where the borders are, how many people are in and around the area, and where homes, shops, equipment and other hunters could be. This method is more dangerous if you don't have all the information and a rigid plan for safety. You don't want to get shot, and you don't want to shoot any unintended targets. DO NOT use this technique without considering every possibility.

If you hunt out west, you try to spot animals from far away, then sneak around, undetected, to where they are or where you think they will be. You can't really do that in Georgia. That's not the spot and stalk that I am talking about. Here is the method I use.

Determine a point of entry on the farm that you want to hunt where you will be walking directly into the wind. You want the wind in your face and never at your back. Using very quiet and accessible routes, you will travel across the farm against the wind. The method is simple. You walk slowly, quietly, and pay attention to every step. Patiently walk 75-150 yards, then stop, look, and listen. (This distance is adequate for more open areas, if it's thicker and you can only see 50 yards around you, cut the distance in half.) Get beside some cover and pause for 5-10 minutes. Once the time has elapsed, if you are seeing and hearing animals, stay there as long as needed or as long as animals are in the area. If you don't see or hear anything, move another 75-150 yards and repeat the pause, looking and listening intently. Repeat this process until you make it across the property or get as far as you wanted to travel. If you arrive at a place with obvious heavy deer activity, stay in those spots longer. The key is pausing frequently. If you are constantly moving, the deer will see you before you see them.

This is an effective way to cover the area with limited scent dispersal, to detect more animals, and to learn valuable scouting information. This may be the way you kill your big bruiser or the way you find a few new honey holes that you never knew about. Carrying a walking stick/shooting stick can be a solid idea so that you don't have to shoot freehanded. For this style of hunting, have a trustworthy set of binoculars, preferably in hand or around your neck. You have to be ready. I walk with my gun in hand, not on my shoulder. Sometimes you will catch a single tail flicker and only have a few seconds to make the shot.

I have killed many deer using this technique. It's exhilarating and probably my favorite way to hunt. It takes practice. Don't do it too often and don't walk through your best areas and risk contaminating them. Travel creek beds, firebreaks, roads, and routes that are easy and quiet. Carefully creep up to food plots and fields to scan for activity.

CHAPTER 15

Supplemental Strategies and Uncommon Sense

MOON

What about moon phases, temperatures, feeding charts, almanacs, barometric pressure, and the other 42 things hunters talk about?

Some people may disagree with me, but I will tell you my honest, simple, experienced opinion on all these issues. I think the almanac and the feeding charts mean nothing. Your grandfather may have sworn by them, but I don't. The chart may say that peak feeding time is 11:40 a.m. in September when it's 94 degrees, but if you sit in the woods, you likely won't see any deer feeding. What I find is that if someone follows the chart and is successful one time, they remember that time forever and seem to forget about the 137 times that the chart was wrong. Do what you want to do, but don't be surprised if the chart leads you astray.

Temperature absolutely affects deer movement. When it's blazing hot, they won't move as much. When it's cool, they will typically be inclined to move more. They are like you and me. They want to be comfortable. A heavy, hairy buck gets hot walking around when it's hot outside, and he doesn't want to be panting and sweating all day. If it's cold outside, that doesn't guarantee movement, but generally speaking, cooler temps are better than hotter temps for increased activity. I have killed superior bucks in hot weather, but those hunts are few and far between and do not compare to the cooler weather hunts.

Does moon phase affect deer activity? Absolutely, but not in the way that most people think. There is a lot of speculation, confusion, and even superstition about moon phases. I don't know what your grandpa told you, but I can confirm that one thing is true. A fuller moon will have more deer activity in the nighttime hours than a completely dark night. It's not because of gravitational pull, ocean tides, or spirituality. It's simply because it's easier to see out there. Deer can see pretty well in the dark but can see much better under a full moon with more light. They tend to be more active when there is more light during the nighttime hours. What does that mean to you? It typically means that you will see less deer on a morning hunt during a full moon because the deer have been up all night feeding and socializing. By the time the sun comes up, they have retired for the day. Sometimes, you can hunt later in the morning during a full moon and watch a deer at 10:00 a.m. instead of 7:30 a.m. because their schedule of feeding and resting has shifted. This is especially true in the cooler months, later in the season.

I have also observed increased activity just before a front moves in. If heavy rain is coming the next day, it seems that deer will be more active before the storm sets in. Some people would argue with me on that one, but I think it's a legit pattern. I have also noted decreased activity immediately after a warming trend comes through.

Take this for what you will, but in general, know that dark nights with cool temperatures are probably your best bet, and that sweltering, fully lit nights are probably the worst.

BIG DATA

Every time you sit in the woods, you will get more data. Every time you pull a camera card, there will be valuable information to learn. After a while, there is so much information that it gets blurred in our heads. I encourage you to keep a spreadsheet on your computer to assimilate all of your data. On that sheet, record the stand location, where you sat, what the temperature was, how many bucks and does you saw, what time they showed up, what direction the wind was blowing, and which direction they were traveling. You can do the same for your trail cameras. After a while, a seemingly random set of numbers can start to turn into a readable, repeatable pattern. You may realize that one location always has tons of does around it. That may be a prime spot to return to for the rut. You may notice that one side of the creek only gets visited by deer in the afternoon, and they always come from the west. Anything that we can learn and potentially pattern will help.

It's also smart to keep a harvest record of every deer taken off of the property. If you keep total doe and buck numbers, record weight, time of kill, and rack size, you can observe how, over time, your management plan is working.

NATURE'S CANDY

If you have persimmon trees, pears, grape vines, or other edible fruits with short seasonal output, use them to your advantage. These trees can be a magnet for deer activity for a week or two when the fruit is ripe. I recommend fertilizing any and all of these trees in the spring so that they make the most fruit. It took me ten years of hunting before I even knew that persimmons existed. After watching the tree pull deer after deer right under it, I figured it out.

DON'T BE A DIVA

It's hard to hunt when it's hot, humid, and buggy. However, Georgia deer typically get into their best patterns in late summer. Don't forfeit one of the best chances of the season because it's hot. The sweat is temporary, but the benefit could stick with you forever. The best hunt I ever had was on a 90-degree day, the first week of bow season, in September. The three shooters were traveling together and showing up every afternoon during hunting hours at one of my spots. I had never hunted the spot before, but the stand had been hung a month before the season, hoping for the right wind. I was bow hunting on opening day, and all three of them, plus six other deer came within 15 yards of my tree. The most mature buck was the last one in line. I watched all of them travel from 400 yards to 15, one after the other, walking right by me. It was unreal! The boss buck received my broad-head in his rib cage about 20 minutes before dark.

Abort Mission

If you get busted heading in or coming out of a stand setup, you may want to consider not using the route again, and maybe even abandoning that stand location. People will say that deer have a poor memory, but I can tell you from experience that they are quite keen on recalling bad experiences. I had a doe and a yearling swing around me one morning and wander directly downwind. That mother doe looked right at me, knowing that I shouldn't be in that tree, and blew out of there, letting the world know that she was upset. She sounded off on every bound, blowing until she extended out of earshot. I hung a new stand about 75 yards away, and two weeks later both of the deer came back. However, this time, the wind was fine. The mother doe stomped all the way in, hyper-alert, looking right at the old stand, trying to catch any movement. She stared and circled for 45 minutes, looking for a reason to bolt out of there. She started blowing again, looking at the stand the whole time. She hadn't seen me or smelled me; she just remembered where she saw and smelled me last time. I decided to fill a doe tag because she knew too much.

TOUGH ACCESS MAY BE THE BEST ACCESS

If there is an area on the property that's hard to get into, and few people ever attempt to hunt there, that's probably where the bucks are. I leased a Georgia farm a few years back. When the prior hunter that leased the placed passed on the property map to me, he told me the borders on each side. He told me that Spring Creek was the western border. That was an accurate statement. However, what most of the previous hunters thought was Spring Creek was actually a small tributary of the creek. Once I studied the maps carefully, I realized that there was a ten-acre island in between the creek and the tributary, and no one had set foot on it in at least five years. I knew that this was somewhere I needed to be, despite the need to cross a waterway that was 4-feet deep and 15-feet wide. I located the shallowest crossing and returned the following day, downwind, wearing chest waders. I held my gun and a spare pair of boots above my head and crossed the shallowest section, which was almost at the top of my waders. Once I crossed over, I pulled the waders off, put on my hunting boots, and entered the area quietly. I kept the wind in my face and walked until I had a decent opening in which I could survey about 80 yards. I quickly and quietly assembled a small ground blind out of sticks and sat down on the ground, my back against a big oak, and my body covered in the sticks. About an hour before dark, a beautiful, mature

10-point came into the area. I had no pictures of him, but immediately knew he was a shooter. He was huge. He stopped twice, but never offered a decent, clear shot. He moved across, and I heard him get into the waterway I had crossed an hour before. I was pumped and disheartened at the same time. I listened to him cross the water and continued to wait. A doe showed up at 50 yards eating acorns, and she suddenly looked up, focusing her attention towards where she had just come from. An awesome 11-point showed up, built like a tank. I shot him at 20 yards, from the ground, before he reached the clearing. This was a deer that showed up once, on one of my cameras a month before, and had disappeared.

The moral of the story is simple. Sometimes we should go where no one else has been, or where no one else is willing to go. I have killed deer in some very inconvenient locations to retrieve it, and not thought about that until afterward, but hey, it's an adventure.

I have climbed embankments, walked miles, walked train trestles, used waders, rode mountain bikes, ridden aluminum boats, and even paddled kayaks to get to a secluded hunting spot. Whatever you do, be safe, and know that the effort may produce a significant reward, especially if no one else is willing to go there.

THINKING OUTSIDE OF THE BOX

I have to tell one more story to illustrate the point that we should be thinking creatively and pushing new methods to get to secluded deer ground. When

I lived in Augusta during grad school, I didn't have a lease or permission to hunt. I elected to hunt public land, WMA's, and hope for invites from friends. There was a section on the Savannah River that sat between two dams. There were no boat ramps and no access for people to get in this section of the river. I carried my kayak from a public park and paddled out to the few islands on this section of the river to hunt ducks. A few buddies and I were each on an island, blasting mallards and ring necks. During the first 30 minutes of daylight, I saw a nice buck swim from one island to the other. It was a cool sight, but I didn't think much of it. The next morning, we were back out duck hunting, and he did it again at almost the same exact time. Now he peaked my interest and spurred my opportunistic nature.

I returned home, called the DNR office and asked about shooting rifles on the river. He said rifles were not allowed, but that shotguns were. I asked about this specific portion of the river and if it were legal to deer hunt with a shotgun. He told me that it was legal, as long as I was on the Georgia side of the state line, but that there were no boat ramps. I double checked the legality. He confirmed it, and I knew what I needed to do. I switched the barrels on the shotgun and placed the slug barrel on it instead of the duck setup. I called my two duck hunting buddies and told them to do the same, and that we would be deer hunting the next morning, and traveling by kayak. I knew which island the deer was bedding on, but didn't know which one he would swim to. Each of us positioned on an island just downstream of the one he bedded on. Thirty minutes after light, he appeared on the bank the same way he had the two days before. He started swimming, and we all wondered which island he would travel to, hoping for a shot opportunity. He swam right to my island, where I was hiding in the brush. He climbed onto the bank, 20 yards from me, shook water off like a wet dog, took one step up the hill, and BOOM, I let him have it!

I know this is a crazy story and one that I will likely never experience again, but I wanted to include it to illustrate that being creative and getting to a spot that no one else disturbs can be very beneficial. I can tell you that paddling a kayak down the river like a Seminole Indian, with a big buck that I had just killed strapped to the front of it, is one of the coolest things I have ever done. I still can't believe that it worked out.

This is the "Kayak Buck" from Northeast Georgia. What an awesome morning.

TIGHT SPOTS CAN HOLD BIG BUCKS

Often, the most undisturbed, non-pressured hunting spots are just inside the property gate, right behind a house or shop, or in a tiny spot that you assume doesn't hold any deer. If there is a place on the property where no people ever bother, it may just be the best place to hunt a big buck. This can also be the case on public land.

Deer sometimes prefer a place where they only have to worry about watching a single direction. You will find that deer will sometimes bed right beside a pond, a highway, a pasture, or an embankment. They take comfort in knowing that nothing can sneak up behind them, and they can relax and just monitor one area in front of them. For example, they will lie down with the creek behind them and face away from it with the wind blowing their face. They relax knowing that if a threatening intruder were to come across the creek, they would hear it, and if one were to come from in front, they would smell it. Use this to your advantage.

KNOW THY WEAPON

A good hunter must be an excellent shooter. Becoming an accurate marksman, and maintaining the skill takes practice. You must be confident in your weapon and your abilities to make the critical shot without any error.

A gun hunter should know, without any doubt, that her weapon is precisely tuned in. Scopes should repeatedly be checked for accuracy throughout the season, and many rounds should be fired to be overly familiar with the weapon and the trigger. It's also vital to know the ballistics data for the particular round that will be fired in the field. Knowing how much the bullet will drop at each possible range, and practicing all possible ranges will prove to be invaluable.

Bow hunting takes even more practice to build needed confidence. Practice arrows should be fired from every potential hunting distance and should be launched from a similar stand setup that will be used for hunting situations. If you hunt from 12 feet up a ladder stand, practice from there too. Constantly test your skills in varying conditions to know what to expect from the arrow flight. A slight wind, a light drizzle, or even heavy humidity can dramatically affect your arrow flight.

Always check your weapons accuracy after travel, especially airport travel. If you accidentally bang it on the truck door or your tree stand rail, check it again the first chance that you get. Keep shooting until you gain the skill set and confidence to perform in a tense, game-time situation without anxiety. Your adrenaline will be pumping enough already. You never want to second guess your skills or equipment in the heat of the moment while staring at your dream buck through the crosshairs.

Code of Conduct

I just want to say one more thing before you head out to bag your buck. Elite Georgia hunters are a bit of an unofficial club. Like a fraternity, sorority, or civic organization, there are expectations of how members will behave. I encourage you to rise to the top of the hunting population and join us at the top, not only with harvest results, but in the way you handle yourselves. Here are the bylaws.

1. Respect the land. Leave it better than you found it. It is a gift and a privilege to live and hunt in Georgia. Be a good steward of nature. Improve the properties you hunt and cause no damage. Don't litter or dump trash on the place. Clean up waste whenever you find it. Do your part to preserve what you have been given so that future generations may enjoy it too.

2. Respect your neighbor. Work together to improve the animal numbers, health, and

vitality. Communicate with each other regularly to find common goals, develop plans, and pool resources to achieve a common goal. Do not trespass or bother anyone else's property, ever. If you need to track a deer that ran across the line or jumped a property fence, get permission first. Good relationships go a long way in hunting careers.

3. Respect the animals. Take ethical, lethal shots, and finish the job as quickly as possible. Do not allow animals to suffer. Make every effort to recover wounded animals. Harvest only the deer that you plan to eat yourselves or donate for others to do so. Do not waste the natural resources that are so precious to our community. Abide by the laws and limits set forth by our Department of Natural Resources, and contribute back to wildlife programs when you are able.

These things have intangible value. Please honor the code and pass on the practice to your apprentices and hunting buddies. Lead by example.

Farewell

I hope that you have enjoyed this book, and I hope that it will enrich your hunting experience. I trust that there has been some level of education that you can use in your journey. These skills and techniques require diligent practice. Be disciplined. Be patient. Enjoy your time in the woods, and savor the fruits of your labor. I wish you well on your quest.

Made in the USA
Lexington, KY
18 December 2017